The Poetry Review

The Poetry Society, 22 Betterton Street, London WC2H 9BX

The Poetry Review

The Poetry Society, 22 Betterton Street, London WC2H 9BX
Tel: +44 (0)20 7420 9880 • Fax: +44 (0)20 7240 4818
Email: poetryreview@poetrysociety.org.uk
www.poetrysociety.org.uk

Editor: Emily Berry
Production: Michael Sims

ISBN: 978-1-911046-06-6 ISSN: 0032 2156
Cover artwork: Sophy Hollington, sophyhollington.com

. . .

SUBMISSIONS

For details of our submission guidelines,
please visit *The Poetry Review* section of
www.poetrysociety.org.uk

ADVERTISING

To advertise, visit
www.poetrysociety.org.uk or
contact Oliver Fox on +44 (0)20 7420 9886,
email: marketing@poetrysociety.org.uk

BOOKSHOP DISTRIBUTION

Central Books, 50 Freshwater Road, London
RM8 1RX, UK. Tel: +44 (0)20 8525 8800
or visit www.centralbooks.com

PBS EXCLUSIVE BOOK SUPPLY SERVICE

Readers of *The Poetry Review* can order books
featured in the magazine by mail order from the
Poetry Book Society. Add 10% p&p.
Tel: +44 (0)191 230 8100
or email pbs@inpressbooks.co.uk,
quoting *The Poetry Review*.

SUBSCRIPTIONS & SALES

UK individuals: £35 / Europe: £45
Rest of the World: £50
(all overseas delivery is by airmail)
Single issue: £8.95 plus postage.
Order from www.poetrysociety.org.uk/shop or
contact Paul McGrane on +44 (0)20 7420 9881.
Pay by cheque (sterling and US dollar
cheques only), credit card or Direct Debit.

The Poetry Review is also available on audio CD.

The Poetry Review is the magazine of
The Poetry Society and was first published in 1912.
A subscription to *The Poetry Review* is included as
part of membership of The Poetry Society. It is also
on sale in leading bookshops. A digital version of
the magazine is also available. Views expressed in
The Poetry Review are not necessarily those of The
Poetry Society; those of individual contributors
are not necessarily those of the Editor.

Charity Commission No. 303334.

Cover quote by Lee Young-Ju, translated by Jae Kim, see p. 24

THEPOETRYSOCIETY

Supported using public funding by
**ARTS COUNCIL
ENGLAND**

CONTENTS

Poems

Gallery

Essay

Poems

Profile

Report

Reviews

EDITORIAL

There is "an undecidability at the heart, at what Coleridge called the inner *penetralium* of the poem", notes George Steiner in his essay 'On Difficulty', which considers what it means to find a poem 'difficult'. It is possible, he points out, for a seemingly obscure poem to nonetheless 'mean' a great deal to us, suggesting that mystery and obscurity can make themselves intelligible in ways we do not quite understand, or have no name for.

In his essay for this issue, Jack Underwood writes in praise of uncertainty, and of the poem as an "open habitation", a place where – instead of looking for answers – one might engage richly with not-knowing amid the unstable, ever-shifting "shoal of jellyfish" that is language and meaning: "Solving the mysteries of the universe: isn't that just the most arrogant, preposterous thing you ever heard?" I suppose the desire to solve a mystery, though, also has to do with fear. If you look up "uncertainty" in a thesaurus most of its synonyms are negative: "anxiety", "confusion", "distrust", "mistrust", "uneasiness"... Politically we live in a time of great uncertainty, where mistrust and unease proliferate. People are not always comfortable with grey areas; bad things can happen in the shadows. Yet it's often clarity rather than uncertainty that poets distrust. The Cuban poet Juan Nicolás Padrón, translated by Louis Bourne, writes satirically of the lost "principle of uncertainty" in 'I Have Hopes of Being a Skeptic', implying that clarity can be a kind of obfuscation – "Now everything is very clear, / and there's such luminosity / that one suffers from accepted blindness" – which calls to mind Mahmoud Darwish's assertion (as translated by Fady Joudah) that "Extreme clarity is a mystery".

What kind of sense can be made of a poem? Veronica Forrest-Thompson has argued that "poetry must progress by deliberately trying to defeat the expectations of its readers or hearers, especially the expectation that they will be able to extract meaning from a poem", while Wallace Stevens wondered, "If the poem had a meaning and if its explanation destroyed the illusion, should we have gained or lost?" But there are kinds of meanings that register somewhere beyond our ability to understand or explain them; there can be a pleasure (and hence a kind of meaning), as Adam Phillips has remarked, in "listening to voices without understanding what they are saying".

A 'penetralium' is the innermost, most secret part of a place or building – a place, maybe, that you can't get to. "That a house rises inside a person, that one keeps forgetting it", writes Lee Young-Ju in Jae Kim's translation of her poem 'Brewery'. The word makes me think of the theory of the "psychic crypt", developed by psychoanalysts Nicholas Abraham and Maria Torok, which denotes an internal space split off from and completely inaccessible to the self, but nonetheless communicating its presence. Of this psychic space, Derrida wrote, "The crypt is enclosed within the self, but as a foreign place, prohibited, excluded." We might think of the topography of a poem in a similar way: as fathomless as a consciousness. "The mind is some next ends", comments Kayo Chingonyi in 'Blues for Albert "Prodigy" Johnson and Carl "Haystee" Samuel', speculating similarly in 'The last night of my 20s' that "Maybe it is better some things / retain their mist / that all of us might carry a well of myth / in the pit of our pith". Wallace Stevens believed poetry's mystery was essential to its nature and its 'meanings' could be discerned only by succumbing to the mystery. "We do not pretend / to know where we are going", chorus the voices in Linda France's 'Morralee Wood'. May we forget our need to make sense of things and find ourselves, if only temporarily (like Richard Georges' speaker opposite), "ecstatic and lost"...

Emily Berry

RICHARD GEORGES

On Remembering, or Dreams of Remembering

I am forgetting myself. I forget myself
    in the rolling cane, knee-high and wondrous,

ecstatic and lost. There was a ravine in Caroni I peered
    into once, it was filled with a gleaming

alligator – its back full of ridges sharp as teeth
    threatening the sky. I forget if these memories

are dreams (I don't know which I should trust more).
    In a torrent, my father and brother move

a sleeping snake. A tree has fallen in the way,
    my father and brother must move it in the rain.

I enter a room. Turn on a light. A tarantula sits
    on my bed, black hairs bristling in the halogen.

He bids me sit. I sit. He raises two rust-tipped legs
    as if in question – *am I home?*

Too Full of Vermouth and Cigarette Smoke

when I leave I want there to be a carpet of poui
        and the scent of fresh dew and longing

rain sweeping into the harbor and over
        the mountains like walls of gray,

my daughters giggling as they are now,
        I am too full to be remembered like this,

goodbye comes in the languages I cannot remember,
        I cannot understand anymore

how many different ways there are to say harvest,
        to feel the coarseness of the seed

on your tongue when the magic of the fruit
        has disappeared with the guinep's flesh,

how you can spit into dirt and grow something
        beautiful. I know I shall be leaving soon, so

let there be seats for the coffee drinkers
        (grounds wet like earth). When I am gone

        do not tell anyone I am gone.

JEN HADFIELD

Mortis and Tenon
for Mike and Gill

When I took the notion to build a gate, gates
grew as I travelled the isles. The idea propagated
gates – gates I'd never noted before.

While I borrowed drills, chisels, clamps, saws,
gates grew as fast as bamboo – lunchbreaks,
I surveyed gates – the spruce portcullis
at the back of Scallwa stirkened
with yolk-thick paint, the hill gate flexible
as a bird's wing; the gate where no gate hung
palpably from strainers at Gossigarth, two
stout trunks stripped by winter, promising
to sprout a gate, come spring. I asked

which way the brace should run to bear
the load of the dragging wing, arguing
the toss for mortis and tenon while on
their hinges, gates, impatient, ached,
until it was known as Gate-gate, and
mine, for a week or two, the most
debated gate in the isles. A second

coat dried. Oval knots blinked through
the paint. And tracked by the godly eyes
of gates, everything fell into place, as mortis
knit to tenon with a tap, like a wooden latch
into its cradle, and gate after gate swept open
its slow and drooping wing –

Quarff
for N.

Between us run the whale-backed hills.

Valley's the last thing the sun can remember
– slapping the foreheads
of west-facing cliffs, their feet in dark pools.

You don't want to leave your seabirds at dusk.

I can't bring myself to enter that vale
where the bluet bull wades a lagoon
of kingcups, ignoring
his cows.

To enter the virkie damp.

To drive through the vatchley gloom.

KAYO CHINGONYI

The Frequency of Longing

Towards the end
when she   drifted   beyond the reach
of human medicine my mother
assembled a necklace of denominations.

Pentecostal   Roman Catholic
Seventh-day Adventist   Anglican
and the African Church   that met in a school
of which   my mother   myself   and the pastor
were the entire congregation.

From this six-month I remember best
a Christian Science Reading Room
in Richmond; Mum leafing through
a copy of *The Monitor* placing her
faith in words lifted to the frequency

of longing   a pitch so lofty
only a celestial ear could bend to it
and, if the ear belonged to a person
or persons outside time, that being,
or those beings, might grant divine
provenance;
                        give my mother a sign.

The last night of my 20s
for Roddy Lumsden

Fitting that the day should dawn
in this most Lumsdenesque of Lumsdenesque
locales: sea-froth for night music
and the company of Suzanna –
kind enough to show me this walk
she knows without recourse to light.

When the hour came
'Mr Brightside' played it in
a song to which
            by dint of the glint
                    in Sophie Barnard's eye
                            twelve years ago
I cannot listen passively.

Which calls to mind the secret canticle
that undoes you, Roderick.
Maybe it is better some things
retain their mist
that all of us might carry a well of myth
in the pit of our pith
maybe it is by such melodies we exist.

Blues for Albert 'Prodigy' Johnson and Carl 'Haystee' Samuel

Another scribe of black trauma has passed
from this life into the spirit world
or nothingness depending on how much
store you set by Nietzsche –
apt that the arch-laureate of nihilism
comes to mind when I think
of Prodigy, old before his time,
as I was old before mine.

                    •

We passed an adroitly rolled zoot
round a circle in Barking
(before it had a health spa).

One of our number was confined,
these times, to his room by shame,
a death of some kind,

because, lying under a sky
pockmarked with stars, he asked
his girlfriend why she was so quiet

in spite of the feverish intensity
of his thrusts. She recited her
favourite maxim: *you cannot
fell a redwood with a hatchet.*

                    •

When Haystee walked
or fell in front of the lorry
did he *pass away*

if I can still hear him
going back to back
with Kaystar and Rapsz
if I think of him
standing shoulder to shoulder
with Prodigy, in a circle
of dead emcees,
screwing up his face
singing:

> *Listen up, I'm so raw-ah*
> *you know I'm MC Haystee*
> *and I'm on tour-ah*
> *when I spit my lyrics*
> *dem a shout more-ah*
> *and when I give you more*
> *the people dem will be so sore-ah?*

.

In the year of our lord
two double oh three
Toks was still passing
himself off
as *Little Dizzee*
though Toks
was by then
closer in height to Jamakabi.

After *Lord of the Mics* dropped
the gas was such
it just took a younger
bussin' a half-decent
beatbox for the clash

to start. Everyone played
their part – from the hype-
men spitting lines back

like a space echo
to the galdem standing
outside the cypher
but close enough
to cuss the vanquished
when a gap opened for him
to walk in the unforgiving
light of mediocrity.

This was before anyone
in our circle had been
stabbed or shifted.
Some had shouldered
a wooden box
but none of us understood
the cost of the shanks
and skengs in our lyrics.

If we knew these days as halcyon
is hard to say.
The mind is some next ends;
we wouldn't have been caught dead
slipping – convinced
as we were the patch of grass
beside The Golden Fish
was big enough to constitute a world.

BILLY RAMSELL

Two Boys
Barcelona, 1995

They hold hands saying nothing.
They return from the ripple-less sea.

They traverse the long, implacable
noon and afternoon
like supple frictionless sunlight

as if their calves, their carved torsos
were manufactured from sunlight,
from wavelengths tanned and tangible.

They know no ignorant byways,
no side streets with stupefied
rancorous men, will enter
neither evidence nor pleading,

and as they amble man-hand
in capable man-hand past
the surf-shops of Admiral Cervera Street

one dips a slow and definite
unexpected kiss to the elbow,
to the strolling muscovado shoulder
of his companion,
takes a lipful of salt from that easiness.

And the butterflies of rumour start absconding:
flakes of hearsay, membranes
barely there but pulsing
in their cornflower thousands

from the colony of notches
on that great pocked wall,

their pigments spelling the future,
telling nothing whatever
will ever be the same again
in all the precincts of Catalonia.

They hesitate, hover amid the Saturday traffic
then in their pullulating spiral
climb the air.

They skim level above the esplanade
and the Museum of National History,
above the two boys

billowing out, out over indolent shallows,
beyond the sleek, gleaming
sloops and schooners
until they're only a blue plume vanishing
until they're lost in a haze of heat and spray

then further fluttering further
as they ride the leisurely thermals
as they're spooled across the teal
and lavender immensities,
their tenuous wingspans breaching
horizon after horizon

straining to reach and reaching
a schedule of quaysides:
petrol-scented docklands
and workshy, terracotta harbours,
beaches that await their butterfly insistency,

then Montpellier, Naples,
yet more distant, shimmering somewheres
that their tidings, their indigo gospel,
their weightlessness
will settle on by morning.

*The opening of this poem adapts several lines from 'Two Girls' by the Catalan poet
Gabriel Ferrater.*

HOLLY PESTER

International Workers' Day

I was put into a rare recovery position
(the shape of bog people in loose rope)
My niece sings a song under her fleece
He only had to peep in, to peep in, but he still couldn't do it
I hand her two lions to put in her cheeks, purple and yellow
There's too much to do around here
What is wrong with her?
I have a dragon problem and need help from the giant story
I pretend to eat a wooden radish – are you selling or is it a gift?
Pretend to kiss the grey spill
That's a real island – they're pointing at my earring
Someone is very small she's crawling over my knees and whispering to her
brother, why did she come here? You cannot move, you mean something else
Not your plot, particular dirt, the plot, its expressive stillness
She fell and slapped her head on my laptop
\, 5   name the poem, devotional shipwreck
Women lie down in various rooms of the house
taken in by an older brother's homeopathic handling
edged up to the dinner table
Glasses in memory of running to another flat with socks on, she's on
the kitchen floor
The *kitchen* floor?
This is the seabed, a melted spine, proto-storytelling
Use the swan-necked spider to get past an obstructing ball
No problem, you guys look great together, I'll just dissolve
This avenue gets more political every time I walk it
William Blake never left town
A man with a gentle Northern voice shouts with real excitement, "Has it
nestled? Has it nestled?" it has
it's soaking

O. FLOTE

Nyanga

Earnit was making chuft with a gwai
giving it careful lipwork weathering smoke into brief clouds

when Dandruff – ordealed from a last-minute witch-hunt of his bachelor's
that led from his being showered and spanked in his Robin Hood

guds by two naked Russians on stage to his betrothed
throwing his clothes and soft porn out on to the verandah

epilogued by a brow-stretching eye-crumpling rally to let be let be
and the wedding on its day he happy at her she just happy –

when, as I say, Dandruff not a day hitched and dusted
pipes up with an overture sigh and lick of his teeth

and starts tuning this episode off his hairy chest:
Yussis, bruh, do you recall that ouen Armpit

(so called because he had established such good terms
with himself that his brother in hair and stare must've been Brad or Cock)

Eesh, breathed Earnit, that family were laaaank godbothering
made Jesus look like an FT in his own backyard!

Jah, d'you remember how they had that cabin up in Nyanga?
Earnit gave a nod, Well, Dandruff went on, Armpit invited me

up there one weekend, we must've been in form 2 or 3
and that first morning I should've sussed the tone

when his old-boet rocked up to breakfast in a paisley gown
flowing open and his porksword swinging at the toast before he sat

and they all bowed their heads and said grace thanks god for bacon
and egg as if all was well. All was not well, bruh, I thanked god

for short-term memory loss but that old-boet's cock so burned
my skull the only forgetting I could do was how the fuck to,

I mean, there he was asking me to pass the butter, almost singing
to himself and his wife suggesting they take a drive to Pungwe Falls or such

and Armpit saying dad and mum as if they were at the PTA;
but when they'd gone, I went back to the manual and pulled myself together

so that when Armpit suggested we take the Jack Russell for a walk
I was factory set, as they say, and ready for a bit of getout the cabin

before another fever hit. We tuned the usual shit, rugby, chicks,
and crossed a stream before we found ourselves in a pine forest,

the ground padded with those needles and cones like ammo
lying everywhere. Then Armpit fell to his knees and I thought

okay, he's got to bother god again, until I checked him call
the dog over and offer him his dick. What!? croaked Earnit

slapping the bench. Jah, and as the pooch tucked in
making ice cream of his balls he looked over to me, who

by now was kicking a pine cone and measuring the length of trees,
and said with an earnestness that couldn't leave me speechless

because I was already booked into that institution well and truly,
he said, It's okay Dandruff, Jesus can't see us in the forest.

So what happened, bruh? Earnit stubbed out his cigarette.
I walked ahead, he caught up later and we had dinner at Troutbeck with
    the folks.

You know, Earnit said laughing, I met Armpit in Jo'burg two years ago:
married, two kids, the lot; said he was breeding Jack Russells in Gabarone.

Dandruff sipped his beer, fuckme bruh, funny how we turned out, hey.
Later, they were joined by Gwat and Stiltskin and proceeded to get
    totally unstitched.

gwai – *cigarette;* tuning – *to tune (to tell, to relate);* guds – *underpants (Robin Hood brand);* lank – *a lot, very much so;* FT – *fucking tourist (or other whites from Europe);* boet/ouen – *guy, dude*

Salisbury Prison, 31 December 1966
extract from My Life as Robert Gabriel Mugabe *by Comrade Diogenes Junk*

The Settlers can give you your old life back, it is what they deal in – the past.
They are experts in subverting all other action to this single cause.
They are witches trading in the spells of the past. A past where they are witches
and manipulators of everything to their cause and benefit.

No, Nhamodzenyika, let me tell this to you now so there is no confusion.
I am not the Settlers' slave consort. Their magic has no effect upon me,
riddles me no more. Long ago I gave up the tractable hopes of the naked haggler
for dignity. I restored my eyes to their purpose which is to see how things really are.

I am not weak, though I do suffer; I am not broken, though I ache so much,
so much it's as if my soul were in fact a body dropped from an aeroplane,
a body which aches twice: first, during the fall in anticipation of death and thereby
experiencing death over and over again; and secondly, after the fall

just before the final death when every broken bone and burst vessel,
every crack in your skull and jaw sings with the pain your soul has already known.
This is the dual pain of imprisonment by those who despise you for being
exactly who you are, who you can only be: the pain of the fall.

But what the Settlers don't know, what they cannot begin to understand,
is that I have every faith in the milliseconds of life I shall gain after I hit the ground
and shatter, just before I expel my last breath. It is during this tiny window of life
that I shall rise up and deal an emphatic blow for my people, for our liberation,

and so destroy the realm of the Settlers for an eternity. I am alive now
like never before, in that fraction of time just before death. (Thanks to you?)
And the lust and righteousness budded from this knowledge is what supplies me
    the strength
to write to you now, my son, and to endure what I am destined to become.

LEE YOUNG-JU, *translated by Jae Kim*

Brewery

They say a house too old becomes human, but the old woman goes down to the basement sometimes. The place is packed with rained-on barrels; pork meat she started slicing but stopped rolls around. Is that why. The legend of a rich and bountiful basement world is sometimes like reality. The old woman straightens a white finger and tries sweeping the rainwater. Dips into the rain and tastes it. What's this sensation. Like a blood-soaked towel dyeing her white hand, this flavor. While cutting the rest of the pork with a well-honed blade the old woman starts giggling. She had thought once the dark, the crimson, love's sensation. Even rotting away it was tasty. They'd been hiding inside her jar-shaped skirt, the pieces of cool flesh. Ground up and spilling onto the floor, even that was nice. Each time, the old woman's basement broadened. Go down the stairs and outside the stairs without stopping and the pigs who'd been crying became the old woman's big and sturdy legs. Once you've come in you have to keep going in. Like sweet barrels thoroughly ripening in agony. The old woman is aware of the fate of cruel invasion. That a breath-holding cry could only nicely ripen and continue forever to deepen. That no one wants it. That a house rises inside a person, that one keeps forgetting it. That the place is so very far and collapses like a dream. A person walking across to a person – that one must destroy the house completely to be able to go. Like so, in the basement, souls that started to go but stopped are drinking, exchanging breaths. The tinge of blood that could be rain or tears reeks. Thought that was love. The souls falter, collide against each other. The old woman who pops open a new barrel is a person prying into the sweet basement legend in a country village not on any map. A person writing her will in the white light through the uninvolved window. What kind of a fossil do you expect will form in a basement too wide to walk across? The old woman's getting big as a large mansion. In the garden, trees having passed through a thousand years grow down and barrels get more and more bloated. I want to visit the lucid forest in the north.

JANG SU-JIN, *translated by Jae Kim*

Tofu Synecdoche

Where does the desert come blowing from

Everyone's lying down. Only Tobi and Cogi, they're walking

Tobi and Cogi throw up at the desert's end

Pretty but nuts. Holding Tobi and Cogi's wrists those young ladies of sleep
followed. In the hospital room and in the hallway, they make a small house
and a flower bed. The fat ball of water that broke in through the living room
window. The light is smudged, it's smudged. All women say the same thing.
Smudged, it's smudged. Plop, falls over. So no one can ever raise it. Hardened
as mummies, sleep

Cough cough, a flower vomits ashen sleep. Sleep is water singed

Woman, in her sleep, thinks of one piece of tofu. To think I can neither touch
it nor eat it...... My good old piece of tofu...... You're far too far away. Above the
silky sunshine-laid table, beside the linen curtain wavering in thin wind. Little
by little you rot in every corner. Weak enough to crumble, this life of a lump

The cat nibbling at horn flowers on the fence, it's suddenly patrolling in the
house. Like the little devil. Shedding hairballs strewn with insects. The cat
lightly springs onto the kitchen table and a little scratches the tofu. With
every sneeze the woman falls more deeply into the tofu

One enormous tofu lump

The woman, inside the tofu, dribble-dribbles away. Eyes closed, from this
edge to that edge. Inside the white tofu she receives the leafy season. The
vines that grow by climbing on the woman, the gloomy comers and goers
brined in mold. Having set out wearing an early winter's coat, the grandma
cuts lengthwise the tofu gone bad and slips out of the season

Going somewhere

PENELOPE SHUTTLE

Gardens where there's no need for a garden

For me, it begins with a grandfather consciousness of Russia
and a difficulty of surnames,
smiles in a local kitchen from my alien gold neighbours
and the gladness of their horses

For me, it begins in the dark regions
of vodka and childhood
where the staircase birds share the flight of the child
and a windowsill mother counts
a thousand years
on her exact tongue of black-blood grief

Or it begins, for me, with a master-sleep
with the dog who understands the breast that wears black,
and the hour when a strange
but better than usual guest
comes to call

For me it begins when I step aside
from my own concerns and the dead look at me,
quiet as thimbles,
they look at me from the hushing handheld sky,
its subdued palaces,
the doors all blue and in the wrong places

For me, it begins there

DAVE MARGOSHES

Pears

Far in the back of the farm, way out of sight
of the house, a miniature orchard of pear,
three trees, old and fruitful, a happy family.
In spring, my mother and I would take the long hike
through the meadow and across a small stream
to visit the eruption of pink fragrance, then begin
to count the days, my mother penciling them off
on the kitchen calendar: the fruit we knew
was growing would be ready in the heat of July.
In June, the small orbs would begin to form, seed
turning into flesh, my mother explained, just the way
I had grown inside her. Incomprehensible,
magic. By early July, the pears had reached full size
and were starting to blush, sweetness reddening
their cheeks, but when we sampled they were
still too hard. Now we were coming every day,
armed with pails just in case, but still too hard,
maybe tomorrow, my mother said, day after day.
But then one morning we found the orchard bare,
leaves fluttering like dispirited flags, a scattering
of spoiled fruit underfoot. This happened
every summer through the early years of my life,
expectation, hope, disappointment, a familiar rhythm.
Boys from town, my mother explained. She consulted
with my father but no trap could be devised,
no altering of our own schedule that anticipated
these boys' bitter thievery. Sweetness in our sight,
then snatched away. We must learn to be faster,
I suggested. No, my mother said,
we must learn how to wait.

JULIA COPUS

Some questions for later

What about you, North Baddesley?
Are the night watchmen there still, performing
their spins and quarter-spins in the hut
at the gates of the chemical factory?
They claimed they could see
right in through my bedroom window.
Look for yourself, they said, pointing.
There it was, three houses along,
the little, high-up porthole of my room.

       That soon had you hurrying home.

I hurried in my sleep to morning-time.
Outside, a wispy day-moon hung
unnoticed, like a torn – no, melting –
rice-paper wafer, over scenes it could neither
alter nor illuminate.

       The way you put it, midnight
       is morning, morning afternoon.

That's how it is. None
of the clocks here
is turning. Not a one.

       (As in – *What's the time, Mr Wolf?*
       It's NONE o'clock!)

In the holidays my flinty shadow
stretched, loping, along your pavements,
and more than once struck laughter
from a street corner.

That was you? I heard it!
The sound flared like...
like shook foil! Flame
from a match.

Sound carries further in summer. Did I mention
this happened beside the Sperrings store?

Where else? The kids
that gathered there. Smoking!

I smoked too, but I did it alone.

O dolor! O me! I walked alone
under a torn, rice-paper moon!

Wrong moon. This was after dark.
And in case you're wondering it was
my vicar-grandfather who gave me the wafers.
I was eight or nine. Next time
I asked for them he growled (no doubt
through the fug of a hangover), *Ask Mrs C.*
Mrs C. was his wife. My grandmother.
Oh sweetie, she said. *You must know*
they're not for playing with. What
would your grandfather say?
The shame of asking. Shame...
"like a white balloon / still rolls its cry /
from room to dusty room"...

But that was elsewhere.
I seem to be drifting away.

No. I see you. And especially
I see the house.

> The house and all it housed.
> The noise that came from it!
> There was talk. (I think
> you didn't know that.)
> In the factory canteen.

What can I say? That it
was a loud house: trumpet,
French horn, violin,
piano, 'cello. Rage.
That bad things happened there.
That they are happening still.
That sometimes it seals itself up, will not
be got into. Other times, the opposite.
It opens and spreads, so that to move
around it requires a greater
elasticity of dreaming.

> And all the locks are broken.
> The bathroom and the loo.
> Your bedroom door.

Yes. And that. But it doesn't
stop me returning.
It might be the reason, even.
Sometimes I do it at will.

> You do it so it feels real!

If I press my ears
till all is seasound, white noise,

that's how the factory's hiss arrives,
and with it the sharp phenol smell
that streamed from the great
chimneys. Into the garden, in
through the open windows.
Escape from the smell was impossible.

    Resistance futile!

A house can get too porous. Everyone
in everyone else's business.
I drew in my horns, developed early
a liking for corners, edges, the hemmed-
in back seats of buses, library stacks.
But tonight I'm younger. I am about
to leave, late, with no
sub in my pocket for Brownies in the squat
mission church on Rownhams Road

    ...where Brown Owl says, *Hop*
    twice around the toadstool!

Yes. I'd forgotten that.

    The usual penance. She has made a note.

And the hall is echoey with the voices
of little girls, the windows set high
like projectionists' booths. Through them, dusk
is turning the sky a brilliant shade of crimson
enriched by smoke from the melting tonnes
of resins, sealants, glues and that sticky
vinyl cling-film Stepfather produced one day
for my mother, with a conjuror's flourish.

It clung to everything!

He thumped the box on the counter,
as if he were presenting her with the answer
to end all answers – which, in a sense,
he was. I have seen these things
many times over. I wrap them
in language and make a gift
of them. But what am I left with? I am left
with the old questions, such as what
happens in the voids, the unlit
spaces, when our backs are turned?
And do the gaps grow in the dark,
unseen, as mushrooms do? *Proliferate?*
If it's true that memory is Janus-
faced and looks to the future I would like
very much to meet its gaze but I
am elsewhere now (as in the famous case
of 'Madame I'); can no longer feel
my arms, my legs, my head and my hair.
I have to touch myself constantly.

This is a true and honest account
of the facts. From such a distance
I am as worn – therefore every bit
as pointless – as that wafery moon,
and like her cannot keep
from coming back. Once again somebody
somewhere is getting away with murder.

HISHAM BUSTANI, *translated by Thoraya El-Rayyes*

The Maestro

The musicians finished playing the symphony. They stood up and bowed before the eagerly clapping audience, then started collecting their instruments. Only the conductor was still troubled. Still agitated. Still tapping his baton against his hand nervously.

I am not yet finished, he said to himself.

I am not yet finished, and little by little batches of people withdrew from the auditorium – their chattering voices getting louder.

I am not yet finished, and clanging instruments returned to their cases disturbing the background.

I am not yet finished, and the piano player smiled at the cymbalist – they were about to go on a date.

I am not yet finished, and he looked at the pages before him – the music still falling from them.

Alone, he stayed behind after they all left and when he lifted his baton he heard the opera house walls collapse – its paintings, mouldings, balconies. He heard high, sweeping waves breaking over the chairs spread out before him.

He waved his baton and sent storms spinning.

Tilted it right so that lightning flashed and thunder struck.

Tilted it left so that rain hammered down.

When the Maestro stretched out his baton over the middle, the music divided to open a path for him and so he walked. And when he reached the other bank, the music closed behind him.

He pointed at the middle again, and returned.

Returned to his podium, collected his papers and exited through the backdoor mumbling:

I am not yet finished.

Night

every day:
he enters my window smooth as a sip of whiskey
lies on my couch gently dimming the colours of the room.

and every day:
I banish him as I switch on the light, and he glares at me – enraged –
from behind the glass.

until:
I decide it is time to bury my head in that short-lived, dream-free death.

then:
he returns, a tame, mute dog with amnesia: wagging his tail beside my bed.

LUCIA DOVE

Distraction in conversation

Have you ever had this experience?

What?
Did you ever have this experience of emotional men telling you their troubles?

No, I have not.
When I grew up in Russia I was very badly bullied.
Have you ever had this experience?

I am watching the tall man at the bar and the slenderness of his pale neck.

Did you ever have this experience?

What? I'm sorry, no.
Is your mother very emotional, right?

Russian women are always very emotional, and superstitious.

He sees me and it's like we are suddenly balancing on a tightrope that has
    been rigged through us.

I turn back to the woman and say my mother is very emotional.
Oy, oy, oy! Why we are always in such turmoil!

from Your Candle Accompanies the Sun *by Sophie Herxheimer*

A reimagining of Emily Dickinson's self-imposed seclusion as an act of empowerment. Published by Henningham Family Press, 2017.

I am celebrated
amongst buttercups
with whom I share
the honour of baking
and making from modesty
a version of a field alive
with silk and blazing hope

Essay

ON POETRY AND UNCERTAIN SUBJECTS

Jack Underwood

The game involved my brother or I climbing on top of something not too high, like a sofa, or a tree stump, and asking Dad to catch us. He would get into position and say "Go on! Jump! I'll catch you" and every time we leapt, he'd back away and let us fall. We'd try it over and over, each time becoming more suspicious, demanding new assurances, squinting and giggling as we scrutinised his face. He'd be already laughing as he said it again, "Go on! Jump! I'll catch you." He never caught us, and never would catch us, and that, we understood, was the whole point.

What we loved about the game was precisely the feeling of being unsure: the naïve, delicious, uncertain tension before the jump: maybe, maybe, maybe this time; even Dad must have wondered if he could hold his nerve indefinitely. Nowadays I get my uncertain tension-feelings most tangibly as a writer, and specifically as a person who writes poems. With poems you have to risk all kinds of small, hopeful, doomed leaps; uncertainty is central to your business. You not only have to acknowledge the innate inaccuracy of language as a system that cannot catch or hold onto anything securely, but also that it's precisely this characteristic of inaccuracy that a poetic, empathetic transaction rests on. Writing poems you don't just look up from your computer screen every so often and remind yourself that endless reinterpretation threatens to destabilise each of the terms you are using, or that those terms are calibrated and reliant upon endless further terms, wobbling, drifting and stunning each other like a huge shoal of jellyfish. Instead, you deliberately build your poem as an open habitation; you have to learn to leave holes in the walls, because you won't and can't be around later on to clear up any ambiguities when the lakes of your readers' lives come flooding up through the floor.

If a poem works it's because you've made it such that other people might participate in making it meaningful, and this participation will always rest on another person's understanding of the poem and its relationship to a world that is not your own. Your own understanding of the poem will evolve over time too, as you reread it in light of your changing world, just as you will find the world altered in light of the poem you wrote to understand a small uncertain corner of it. With poems, you never get to settle on a final meaning for your work, just as you never get to feel settled, finally, as yourself. So it seems entirely natural to me that poets, exploring and nudging such unstable material, foregrounding connotation and metaphor, and constantly dredging up the gunk of unconscious activity over which they have no control, might start to doubt the confidence, finality, the general big-bearded Victorian arrogance of certainty as it seems to appear in other forms of language: mathematical, religious, political, legal or financial. I've reached a point now where I'm so used to accepting how flimsily language in poems relates to the world that I can't help but feel appalled at the hapless trust we place in other kinds of language elsewhere. Surely all of meaning and knowledge is apprehended, expressed and configured unstably, is just as much a shoal of jellyfish? Surely we should be uncertain about practically everything?

Before the beginning – unknown.
As after the end – unknown.
But floating, stretched between,

the mind's harmonic mappings,
frail as gossamer,
costing not less than everything.

I am alive. I'm human.
Get dressed. Make coffee.
Shore a few lines against my ruin.

That's Anne Stevenson, at the end of her long poem *A Lament for the Makers* (2006), which imagines that hell is only for poets. "Before the beginning – unknown. / As after the end – unknown." This idea of an overall, timeless uncertainty is not new, by any means, especially when it comes to poetry and different philosophies of language. Poststructuralism in particular has had this covered for over fifty years, and I've waded uncertainly through enough of that to know the limits of my own understanding. Elsewhere, feminist theory has exposed how the Western history of human knowledge has been dominated by white, male knowers, making our so-called 'universal claims' according to finalised, standardised terms, spoken from our supposedly 'objective' perspectives, as if somehow our minds pertained towards to a special clarity and coolness, like water fresh from the fridge.

But it is poetry, not theory, that makes me want to see if the empathetic negotiation of meaning between poets and readers, which is innate to the effectiveness of poetry, is also a dynamic feature of other fields. I want to see uncertainty being put to good use elsewhere, and the most honest approach I can think of is to go about this blindfolded, hands out front, guided by the various furniture I stumble across. Like Picasso said: "If you know exactly what you're going to do, what's the point in doing it?"

I'm not sure I trust overarching theories that know where they're headed in any case, and I dislike the idea of having anything like a last word on a subject. I'm also generally impatient with the way big ideas have to be gradually developed and explained in groaning detail. To understand the really big ones you have to read book after book, become familiar with the shorthand necessary to travel long intellectual distances. Expansive knowledge of this kind accrues like mineral deposits in a cave. There were times as a research student when I thought I was at least inside the cave, but now I feel I am definitely not inside the cave. I think I stole some of the minerals, though perhaps not the valuable ones, and though I remember what it felt like to wander round in the dark with my torch, it's hard to distinguish between what I learned as a slow and impatient reader of theory, and what I have come to understand merely by using and scrutinising language as a practitioner, in life and in poems.

In her 'Short Lecture on Socrates', the poet Mary Ruefle introduces Socrates' "only true wisdom": "knowing that you know nothing". She writes:

> I am forever telling my students I know nothing about poetry, and they never believe me. I do not know what my poems are about, except on rare occasions, and I never know what they mean. I have met and spoken to many poets who feel the same way, and one among them once put it this way: "The difference between myself and a student is that I am better at not knowing what I am doing." I couldn't put it any better than that if I tried.

We all encounter stalling moments of uncertainty when the strategies we have developed for ourselves and each other fail to console the overwhelming complexity and unpredictability of being alive with everything else on earth. At these times we tend to look upwards in the hope that God, or the seemingly omniscient physics of the universe, will disclose to us the Truth, the reason, the theory, its ointment:

> *Please*: a word so short
> it could get lost in the air
> as it floats up to God like the feather it is,
> knocking and knocking, and finally
> falling back to earth as rain,
> as pellets of ice, soaking a black branch,
> collecting in drains, leaching into the ground,
> and you walk in that weather every day.
>   (Ellery Akers, from 'The Word That Is a Prayer')

What interests me about poetry is that rather than looking up for answers, it tends to lead us back indoors, to the mirror, as if seeing ourselves reflected within its frame, confused, gawping, empty-eyed and scalded by circumstance, might re-teach us the lesson: that meaning presents itself precisely as a question – therefore, you can't entertain it by seeking to answer it. Imagine! The old, old universe, arranging itself legibly into a puzzle that our small brains might be qualified to solve with the knowledge we can accrue from our small corner of its tablecloth. Solving the mysteries of the universe: isn't that just the most arrogant, preposterous thing you ever heard? The idea of there being some sort of Answer to Everything is both an admirable feat of imagination and displays a woeful lack of it.

But poems use language so unstably they remind us that the concept of meaning in the universe belongs only to us, and not, in fact, to the universe itself. Meaning is a human beloved: we are literally *made for each other*; no one understands us like we do. So it's as a poet that I feel relatively qualified in my not knowing, and my knowing I don't know, because I spend so much time within that odd intellectual hollow, where words will always fail me. Like Ruefle I also teach poetry for a living, so I guess I am also in the business of teaching my students not to know, and teaching them to understand how and why they cannot know, and to regard this as the "only true wisdom", that is, to see not knowing as a crucial advancement of knowledge. It's really the only kind of knowledge we were born with, and we spend our lives forgetting and remembering it.

But this argument is very abstract; it's got no things in it, and things are of great importance and interest. Of things, Jung says: "if a man does not know what a thing is, it is at least an increase in knowledge if he knows what it is not", which is one of those quotes that feels very helpful, but also, immediately, not so helpful at all. Jung's things are too abstract as well. But we can take from this, by implication, that poetry, unburdened by the need to demonstrate knowledge in a way that is quantifiable or provable, is free to explore the world of things in a way that relies just as much on dissonance or absence as coherence, or evidence. In poems, the foggier aspects of language, which most of the time we ignore or squint through in order to swap workable sentences with one another, are instead called upon deliberately to blur things, to describe things Impressionistically; from across the room a sentence might denote a bridge, a pond, some water lilies, but up close, as it is in poems, language becomes paint again: gestural, layered, the awareness of illusion is part of the effect:

Here is where an afternoon eats its meal from the hollow of elbow pits.
(Momtaza Mehri, from 'Asmura Road, NW2')

Poetry is a deliberate act of foregrounding language, smudging it, to signal possible meanings beyond the everyday, sharper constraints that words and sentences usually afford us, or rather, we afford to them. We know that language is being foregrounded in poetry because often enough we can recognise a poem immediately on the page. Poems tend to announce or frame themselves, either as discrete items surrounded by white space, or else by some other unusual formal arrangement. Form is part of the ceremonial dress code, as if language is putting on some nice white robes to mark itself out as different from the congregation, or it's like in films when people recede on a dance floor to form a circle, making room for someone who has something specific to say by their dancing. With the exception of the poems that deploy a prose-line, usually the page recedes from around a poem, making extra room for the spatial specifics of its performance. But poems foreground their uncertain language in less visible ways as well.

Usually we tend to read texts in a single direction (left to right, top to bottom, in the case of most Western languages) and poems also appear to take place in this same predictable sequence, aside from some notable Modernist or avantgarde exceptions. We are encouraged to trust the standard technology of a sentence, even when it's chopped up into lines, or musically interrupted by great clanging rhymes every ten syllables. But if we look closely it becomes clear that poetic language often operates against the sequential logic of the sentence it inhabits and comprises. For example, when Plath compares her father to a "bag full of God", she asks that the properties of both the father and the bag full of God be examined simultaneously, interchangeably. The words stay fixed in their position in the sentence, but the mind hops back and forth, overlapping the ideas that the words assign, smudging their meanings out of order. The act of comparison, central to poetic thought, antedates the sequential logic of a sentence.

Then there's the fact that poems are commonly held to be rereadable objects, so the whole longer sequence of the poem gets played over, looped, layered, taken out of order; the sustain pedal is held down, until the individual notes become the one great chord of the thing, reverberating. Metaphor, symbolism, music, irony: connotation floods the banks of a sentence so naturally and regularly that language must surely have evolved with these extra breaching, poetic qualities as integral to its working. Without this propensity to overflow, any act of communication would be stunted, cold, robotic, and yet we hardly ever credit this unstable stuff with making knowledge possible, but tend to insist instead that ideas are most clearly communicated through orderly syntax, correct grammar, a breadth and specificity of vocabulary. The epistemic value of poetry has been shunted way down the pecking order. You may as well cough into a hedge and wait for a fact to fall out, that's how our culture feels about poetic knowledge.

> It is very romantic to be a poet...like having a bad back...

> But it is also a pleasure...like squeezing your legs together...and
>   buttoning your blouse all the way up...

> But then it is too much pleasure, like peach pie

> and it becomes...too average to live...

That's Chelsey Minnis, from her book *BAD BAD* (2007), in which she also says things like "Poetry is made to produce an expensive drowsiness... / With a true flickering of disinterest..." or "When I write a poem it's like looking through a knothole into a velvet fuckpad...". If you accrue knowledge through Minnis's poems then it is untethered, fractious, annoyed at being made to sit still. It's a knowledge that wants you to quit being so grabby all the time. An uncertain knowledge. Or take this, from Morgan Parker's 'The World Is Beautiful But You Are Not In It':

> [...] I am getting close
> enough to the sun to touch the tip of its cigar.

> We carry what is shocking and heavy in blood.
> Music seems brighter: the sky the sky.

What to do with a sky that is itself twice over? You can't paraphrase or simplify the complexity of this speaker's predicament. You can't know the shock and weight of the knowledge they carry, instead it's kept bloody, hidden. But this is not the kind of hiding or confusion of elements that shuts you out. It gets you wondering, doing the imaginative hard work of empathy, the heat of that sun, its cigar-tip crackling, the sky doubly wide-open, and something shocking, mortal, weighing down on a collective memory of trauma. Can you feel it? Can you understand? Almost. Maybe. Not something definite, but definitely something.

   This is the kind of uncertain knowledge made possible in poems. I don't mean uncertainty as indecision, but as a philosophical, empathetic stance: I am uncertain. Most poems take this stance in one way or another, and of course there is a wider avantgarde tradition and conceptual field of poetics where meaning in a text can be viewed as a secondary or entirely incidental feature of its construction. But what these various poetries have in common is a resistance to finality in language, and to the kind of certain knowledge that shuts down revision or discussion, or suggests that knowledge can't also be (say it) *felt*.

But it can't just be poems where uncertain knowledge is openly recognised as productive and beneficial. I am sure that if we look we will find that every field of thought employs language that either includes poetic features, or else lives in denial of the inevitable gap that must exist between the word and the thing, it's just that with poetry, and art in general, we are encouraged to feel safe enough in our uncertainty to admit the "true wisdom of not knowing" to ourselves. If we look at humankind's moth-like progress towards the front porch light of knowledge it is typified not by the subtraction of falsehoods to a single strand of Truth, not by a reductive fundamentalism, but by the production of more and more gestures of certainty in different directions. More and more versions of Truth, more and more sources of light on the porch.

We can choose to ignore the noise of other people's certainties with a close-minded conviction in attending to our own; we can rig up a contraption of agreement and say we all see it one way, pretending that there is not enough discrepancy in the small print of our subjectivities to prove this a lie, or we can simply admit that Truth in the Universe Knowable to Humankind is really a great diversification of certainties, crystallising endlessly away from a mythical absolute. Knowledge is, at very best, infinitely Venn-diagrammatic. If art has anything like a duty to the rest of human thought, perhaps it is to remind us that the more versions of the Truth we declare, the less absolutely true our Truth can be.

And since I'm already on my horse, and am prone to finding advantages, I might also suggest that poetry, that oft-maligned, wafty corner of dynamic not-knowing, that shadowy Hamlet mooning around on his platform at midnight, strung out, self-effacing, and spoken to by ghosts, should be acknowledged as the prime medium for the articulation of our knowledge of the unknown.

Uncertain knowledge is declared and revealed everywhere in poetry: "the glass and salt my crooked pathway; impassable glass and salt", writes

Rachael Allen impassably in her poem 'Kingdomland'; "We talk about how weird it is / to be 'a thing'" writes Stacey Teague in 'it becomes a part of –', and I guess Jung would say that this "is at least an increase in knowledge", while Chloe Stopa-Hunt explains in 'Harbour-Chapel' that, "We all decode our blows; what light is, / What vessel, what heart is" and we can only feel our way to believing her strangely, as we feel our way to strangely believing Don Mee Choi, who writes in 'Weaver in Exile', "Dear Father, I am sitting on crows' backs that wobble with grease. Stars look like pebbles from here." And e.e. cummings, what does he have to say about it all?

what's beyond logic happens beneath will [...]

[...] the thing perhaps is
to eat flowers and not be afraid

Eat the flowers and do not be afraid, of uncertainty, of doubt, that seems key; that seems to be what poems are proof of: a fearlessness towards, or defiance against the profound inaccuracy of our perceived reality and relation to it. In 'On the Surface of Things', Wallace Stevens writes: "In my room, the world is beyond my understanding; / But when I walk I see that it consists of three or four hills and a cloud". Of course, he's oversimplifying things to show us, by the inadequacy of his limited scenery, the impossibility of the task in hand, the task of trying to describe what it's like being alive in the world. Oof! It hurts your guts just thinking about it. But then, being brave, staring it down if only for a moment, you can tell yourself what Sophie Robinson does, so restoratively, in 'Hurtface (after Ceravolo)':

o bum! o joy! o bloated world!
    what dreams i am on the stairs of!

Sometimes I get a whooshing-out feeling, a kind of abstraction or self-consciousness about being, especially in large groups of people. I don't think this is unusual. I'm pretty sure most people get feelings of sudden distance from their surroundings for no apparent reason, but with friends, having a nice time, this distance can be entirely pleasurable, sublime even. Someone I love will be talking, or dancing with someone else I love, and in a way I can only describe as cinematic, the volume, or context, drops, and there it all is, this unstable, miraculous wad. I realise I have no answer for it, nothing to say, no conclusion to draw, and yes, I feel something like tranquillity, but also awe, a happy, overwhelming fear. The lack of an explanation for all the wide mad fuss of the world only makes it the bigger miracle: "How – I didn't know any / word for it – how 'unlikely'..." as Elizabeth Bishop puts it in her poem 'In the Waiting Room':

> I said to myself: three days
> and you'll be seven years old.
> I was saying it to stop
> the sensation of falling off
> the round, turning world,
> into cold, blue-black space.

What tethers us down seems so plainly tenuous, so "unlikely", that I think every now and then we should want to fall into that "cold, blue-black space". It seems so arrogant to dismiss its emptiness as unremunerative, or mistake it for an impasse. We know that there's nothing to be found out there, but we can still feel ourselves stood upon the precarious ledge of an inconsolable question together. In poems we can look down at the sheer, deathy drop of it. "Go on! Jump! I'll catch you."

This is an edited extract from NOT EVEN THIS, a book-in-progress of seven essays about poetry and uncertain knowledge.

JUAN NICOLÁS PADRÓN, *translated by Louis Bourne*

I Have Hopes of Being a Skeptic

I have hopes of having a doubt,
though it be only a lukewarm shadow,
but clarity invades.
What can make one falter,
facing a reality so concrete,
against total incandescence?
The principle of uncertainty
belongs to old times,
those that offered a margin of suspicion.
Now everything is very clear,
and there's such luminosity
that one suffers from accepted blindness.
There's nothing to see here.
Now what is seen was observed
by those that had to see.
I have hopes of being a skeptic,
at least of having a doubt,
a doubt that keeps me company
and doesn't leave me so alone.

The Wait

We were a multitude waiting,
but patience ran out.
After the first difficulties,
many gave up.
We resisted at that time
any cyclical catastrophe,
till the worst sacrifice arrived:
we had no idea what we were waiting for.
Some of us persisted,
despite the uncomfortable position
of continuing to wait for something
without knowing what it was.
It rained, cleared and rained again:
the power of water could not erase
the anguished years of so much waiting.
But then we knew what we were not expecting.

MARK WALDRON

WW1 Marcie

Professor Hydrofoil isn't a hydrofoil this morning because
he's a zeppelin, and he's droning over Kent, carpet bombing

Marcie to give us all "something creaky to rub up against".
His incongruous behaviour isn't a disguise, but more of

a contrived mishap. Marcie catches his round bombs
(un-pocked despite aeons of stiff kisses) in her apron which

she holds out as though she meant to collect pommes.
She smiles up at the professor, as she catches glimpses

of him through the leaves, and he looks smiling down
on her like God. Kent and the whole of England roll away

swooning dreamily, cocooned in an intoxicating mist of
honeybees and pollen that's filtered through a timorous

and edgy sensibility, to produce an even more intoxicating,
somewhat paler mist of a quite humongous potency. Back in

the Dog and Duck, Marcie racks up the round bombs that are
all the germane elements of her summer's morning, and cueing

up on the green baize she then breaks emphatically, which the
bombs, of course, adore. *Clack clack-clack-clack!* She pots the lot,

rumble, rumble, clunk, rumble-rumble. Marcie and her fuzzy friends
look appalled that the table should have scoffed everything.

Angry with Trees

What shameless cheats
the trees are.

How poker-faced with
their unbeatable

hands of identical cards,
an uncountable flush

thrown down on the baize
with an obnoxious flourish

just as each card
with its oft-repeated green

turns red and brown
and yellow and orange,

and the trees gather up
their winnings by sucking

the poor ordinary ground as
they get ready to play again.

Well fuck you, trees.
I never met a blasted tree

that didn't have my taste
stuffed in its

wood mouth
like an ace in the hole.

KATHARINE TOWERS

Nonchalant

A robin tinkers with a few odd notes in the hawthorn.
He doesn't mind about autumn.
Non lui chaut – Old French, which means it matters not to him

like the soldiers in *La Chanson de Roland*, who don't mind about dying.
A red leaf trickles slowly through the foliage.
Making no fuss, it lieth quietly down.

LINDA FRANCE

Morralee Wood

Moss

We won't be told who we are – clamp
  our hands over our ears and sing.
    We are fringe and tassel, patchwork

of quilts stitched with our own fingers
  and thumbs. We make ourselves over
    and over, starting again every day.

Flagpoles for the wormed and the winged –
  is that what we are? Doll's house figures?
    The world's smallest ladders to heaven?

Fallen stars? O we are thousands!
  Our code encrypted, low to the ground.
    Light comes and goes, a tarnished spoon.

Gall

We find ourselves blind, invaded, injured
  and so grow strange and outlandish,
    spit out a gob of crabbed twigs –

a witch's broom – make room for the uninvited.
  Say it's evolution: how we work round time,
    beside it, despite it. Prey to parasites

elbowing for survival, puckered and rusted,
  we sprout horns, pustules, spark spangles,
    knuckled cones. Say it's penetration:

how we're sucked dry and poisoned. Our fruit
   the apple – our bastards, twisted,
      streaked with their fathers' sins.

Burr

This land's got its hooks in us. Nowhere
   else to go. Seed, flower and fruit –
      the curse of metaphor, curse

of words black as lead. Falsehood, scandal.
   Our hair stands on end. The stain
      of bad blood saddens our clothes.

We grow on disturbed soil and replenish it,
   mend ourselves. We do not pretend
      to know where we are going,

carry our medicine in the same purse
   we keep our wounds. Brazen, inventive,
      we open ourselves to the horizon.

CARRIE ETTER

And On that Morning I Awoke Whiter than the Night Before

My darling, when a white cop
kills a black man in America,

I am in 1992 Los Angeles;
I am the 23-year-old white woman who

hired the black woman who
isn't working out, and so I

am the one whose choice,
whose error nourishes the prejudices of

my boss, her boss at the small, white firm.
Darling, it is 1992 in Los Angeles,

and one riotous April night I look from west
to east down Santa Monica Boulevard

and see a distant wall of black smoke.
I obey the curfew; I fall asleep

by eight o'clock, never more tired,
only to wake freshly trembling at

these white, white hands.

Heroin Song 3

At the wedding, she explained why everyone should forgive her. Ah, heroin, your sinuous logic in my sister's small head. She arrived sunburnt (sunburnt may be figurative). While her daughter loitered away the time in a nearby town. My sister tells. She wants to tell. There's no palpable apology I can take between my fingers. And if my fingers itch for it? Her eyes are still the blue of periwinkle.

IAN HUMPHREYS

touch-me-not

this flower
doesn't belong
on the canal
hiding
in an airless tunnel
where no one goes
before dark
rooted
to a thin layer
of dirt
head bowed
butter bloom
an open mouth
that faint smell
of sherbet
when someone
passes
it brushes
a thigh
springs back
against the wall
careful
just one touch
triggers
a scattering
of seed
into the night

Bare Branch

I once knew a woman with fine elbows.
       She was visiting her dead grandparents.
On tiptoe she swayed in the bamboo grove, watchful
       as I tiled the roof of my new house.
Uncle read my face... foretold marriage
         and a son with builder's hands.

This woman did not smoke; I liked that.
       She made me bitter melon soup. Old style.
I studied her methods of washing rice, dicing
       pork; her strong, clean hair.
She was not too fat, not too thin.
         She wore purple running shoes: Adidas.

One morning, the woman pointed to the road.
       It floods in winter and the village rests
alone *for months, she said. What would we do then?*
       Repair uncle's pigsty, I replied. Chop kindling.
Perhaps mah-jong
       if we can find a fourth player.

Like others before her, she was no gambler.
       She boarded the weekend bus
to Shanghai, found a job dusting iPhones. In spring
       she returned with a husband who worked
on an assembly line – making buttons
       for Samsung tablets and iPads.

That man has the hands of a woman, uncle laughed
       into his cracked shaving mirror.

How can he build her a home? I invited them both
　　　　to play mah-jong and suffered
a tension headache. Each shuffle of the tiles clattered
　　　　　　like tiny feet through the house.

In China, a 'bare branch' is a man who neither marries nor fathers children and so does not add fruit to the family tree.

VISHVANTARA

My Middle Tongue

I was in my time of grief, and couldn't
hide the fact. My middle tongue, the one
now sprung on a hair-trigger, went and told
Carey Clint right out: children had been
denied me. Though I kept Cock Robin Cottage
clean as a spoon for Dan, I'd always wished
that babbling voices charmed the dust and ash.
Our newest neighbour bowed and raised his cap.
No doubt you've heard by now, how much changed
the day he moved to our Lane. "Forgive me, please,"
I kept sobbing, in between the tear-storms.

A patient horse-cart waited with the last
of his belongings. I had always wished
to feel I made a difference to the lives
around me, and had doubted I could keep
my questions down, and spirits up. But then
he told me all about my middle tongue
that outstared grief; that one which, though I hardly
noticed it, kept silence, so my upper tongue
could blab as usual to Dan. He'd not
refer to a lower tongue, of course. I later
dreamed of it, that such a thing existed!

I slightly turned the ring on my left hand
against my skirt. He hoped the weather held,
then left me as though drenched by baptisms
in which strange voices called me by new names.
Since that day, my middle tongue will whisper
not to mind if things aren't spick and span.
And then we smile, my middle tongue and I,

soft-click to geese, sing hens asleep, startle
ourselves with shocks of wakefulness while Dan
sleeps pink as daisies after sun's descent,
and owls cry wobbling tales to the thin dark.

PAUL BIRTILL

Quick Exit

It's typical really,
I haven't been invited to a party
for twenty years and when I finally
get to one they're all in their seventies
and eighties, except the vicar who was twenty-two.
The host kept saying "The girls haven't arrived,
the girls haven't arrived" and then they did –
all on sticks, which they tapped on the floor
as the vicar did a strange solo dance to 'Tragedy'
by the BeeGees.

Grand National Day

I met him in the street
and asked him if he was putting a bet on.
"No, I can't," he said, "I'm a vegetarian."
What's that got to do with it, I thought –
people have always got to be something.
I remember the year the IRA disrupted
the race and the horses watched while
all the people ran.

JOANNA GUTHRIE

Fort Lauderdale Bus Station

Olive spent till 4 a.m. telling me about The New Jerusalem
which is three hundred and forty-five miles square and twenty storeys deep
with a plot of land each, from which no one will ever steal.
In any case, everyone will be recast in Jesus's image
except for me: I will be trapped on Earth for a thousand years
while Satan rages round, because of how I live.
I plugged in my headphones and let Duke Ellington
erase me, but Olive woke me up
by prodding the soles of my feet from her end of the bench
to describe the pustules in which I will be covered as well,
from head to toe, this being the wages of sin. I needed her on side:
the security guard thought I was looking after her so let us stay,
but eventually I told her, I wasn't raised like that. She said, *You mean*
you stand in your own light? God might make allowances for that.
He'll find you a space, she said. *You don't deserve to burn.*

·

It turned out the security guard ran his SUV as a taxi
to help with the price of gas. He'd drop Olive at the hospital,
she was eighty-five and on her own, then take me to the Amtrak.
The city slid by through tinted windows, I stared at the backseat
full of crap he was storing for other passengers;
McDonald's vouchers on the dash, him huge and fat,
watermelon bubble gum squeaking blue-pink between gold teeth
as he told us how he feeds the birds outside the station every morning.
He said they know him now, and sit on his arm.
When we were alone, he straightaway told me
I raise giant snakes. That's what I do, on the side.

He said back home he had a twenty-eight-foot python. *I raised it from a baby.*
What's she like? *Aw, she's very sweet, y'know.* Softly. *Sweet-natured.*
In downtown traffic, people not giving an inch to let us in,

he said *See? That's what I'm talkin' about. Why they have to hold on like that?*

When we finally found the train, he gave me his card:

> **EXECUTIVE PROTECTION**
> **McBride, T.A.**
> **Enforcement Officer, FL**
> **Commercial/Residential Armed Services**
> **Bodyguard – Plain Clothes**
> **Escort, Landscaping, Patrolling Area**
> **Reconstruction, Buildings, Tents,**
> **Homes, Special Events and Parties.**

It had a little picture of praying hands.
You should have mentioned the snakes, I said
and he laughed, showing all his gold.

•

The TV in the station waiting room was showing food riots:
somewhere abroad the price of rice had doubled in a year.
When the train lit out, it was a sudden cutting away –
the relief of wild thickets of palm, lily-pad pools,
stubby soft pines, leaves with pink tips and white herons
amongst the cattle who grazed their way across the flat green pastures
where a sign said **BEEF – IT'S WHAT'S FOR DINNER**. This
was near to a citrus works, its open-back trucks lined up
brimming with oranges which shone colour to the sky, standing in their own light.

WILL HARRIS

SAY

A brick-sized block of grey stone washed ashore on which was carved
the word *SAY*. My dad picked it up at low tide and two months later found
another, and another saying *LES*. We worked out that rather than a command –
like Rilke's *flow* – it was the name of an old firm, *SAYLES*, which sold
refined sugar, with plantations in the Caribbean and a factory in Chiswick.
As capital flows, accumulates and breaks its bounds, so too had *SAYLES*
broken into various subsidiaries. Slipped, dissolved and loosed. You find
all kinds of things at low tide. One time, a black retriever came wagging up
to me with a jawbone in its mouth. What can't be disposed of otherwise –
what can't be broken down – is taken by the river, spat out or lodged

in mud. The SAY brick took pride-of-place on our chest of drawers –
masonry, defaced by time, made part of the furniture. My dad decided
to give it to you, in part because you're an artist and he thought it looked like
art, but also, which is maybe the same, because it suggested reason
in madness, and made him – made us – less afraid. Last week, there was an
acid attack. Two cousins, assumed to be Muslim, having torn off their
clothes, lay naked on the road, calling for help. Passers-by crossed the street.
Things break, not flow; it is impossible, however lovely, to see the whole
of humanity as a single helix rotating forever in the midst of universal time.
Flow, break, flow. That's how things go. Is it? *What are you trying*

to say? After the operation, they stapled shut his stomach. As the scars
healed, it became harder to discuss. He drank as if he had no body – nothing
said, admitted to or broken. Flow, break, flow. Gather up the fragments.
Now he is back to saying *The country's full. Why are they all men?* Four months
ago, in a flimsy hospital gown, the fight had almost left him. In a tone
you'd use to distract a child, the nurse told my mum about her holiday to
Sumatra in the early '90s. He likes custard, she replied. We told him when
to cough and when to breathe. He clasped a button that controlled
the morphine. Bleep. Bleep. What did the blue and green lines mean?
The sudden dips? What was the nurse's name? I chose not to

keep notes. Thoughtful as moss or black coffee, or as the screen of
a dead phone. That's what eyes look like when you really look at them.
Inanimate. Moss, though, is alive enough to harvest carbon dioxide,
to grow. Yesterday I googled *thoughtful as moss*, thinking it was from
a Seamus Heaney poem, but only found a description of the poet
"grown long-haired / And thoughtful; a wood-kerne // Escaped from
the massacre". At school, we learnt that wood-kernes were armed
peasants who fought against the British in Ireland. I imagined them
(and him) as thoughtful kernels, seeds that had escaped death by being
spat out. I am nothing so solid or durable. *What are you trying*

to say? For years I made patterns in the air, not knowing what to say,
then you came and pointed out the paintwork cracked and bubbling
on the wall beside my bed which, though it stank, I hadn't noticed.
The streetlight sparked on beads of damp. Your skin smelt bready, warm.
I couldn't say how bare my life had been. The stillness in the room
was like the stillness in the air between the heaves of storm. We flowed
into and out of each other, saying – *what?* Saying. Not yet together,
we were incapable of breaking. Cradled in pure being. The paint flaked,
exposing streaks of poxy wall. I remembered a church where the saints'
faces had been scratched away, taking on a new expression: alien,

afraid. Some days I must look alien to him. Scary. One poet said
the devil was neither *blate nor scaur*, incapable of being scared. I sleep
scared most nights but feel no more holy. Once I pronounced "oven"
often like my mum does, and a friend laughed. The cracks appeared
beneath me. In the years before we met, though I wrote, I was too scared –
too scarred – to speak. Flow, flow, flow. I wanted to be carried along, not
spat out or upon. That SAY brick picked from the riverbed proved that
broken things still flow. *What are you trying to say?* When you asked
me that I closed my laptop, offended. Why? It never mattered what
I said. Whether you speak up or scarcely whisper, you speak with all

you are. To the eye of a being of incomparably longer life – to God
or the devil – the human race would appear as one continuous vibration,
in the same way a sparkler twirled at night looks like a circle. In darker days
I couldn't say that to my dad, slumped in front of the TV with a mug
of instant coffee. Saying it now only makes me think of times I've held
a sparkler – the hiss and flare, the after-smell – which runs counter
to that whole vision. One morning, gagging on his breathing tube,
he started to text my mum, but before he could press send his phone
died. He couldn't remember what he tried to say. I can't remember
what I tried to say. Flow, break, flow. You hear me, though?

MELISSA LEE-HOUGHTON

Heroin II
for Robbie Grounds

A life bereft of 3 a.m. birdsong would be a tyranny of sunless misery. When the
    sun comes up it's all done and you are there now
fevering with me, and beside me I have a sense of selfless self that was kept back
    in the stalls with a raging boner for a life-that-could-be
no-longer-excruciating. I breathe lightly, a rattle of falling in, and now no deeper
    to fall we sit in a manky beer garden slugging an eyeful of each other;
and how I want to drink it and swallow it. It comes only ever so rarely, a true
    huge feeling of *all of this.*

I'd get into a chasm without you to heave ho with my night-time; goes on forever
    love, no off-switch with me, and you climb on
and don't hold back from falling in. I get revved up, but it's the filling of all the
    hollow I most want, you are the exact opposite
of endless grief. No, I don't overshoot. My life was its own hovel, now we have
    the flowering of lights and sheepskins. Trouble,
the green juice, and the rattle, the gallon of water it takes to get you through
    a seventy-two-hour hell. I wrap up in a red wool blanket,

your cock asleep in its warmest sleeping memory of purring and hardening. The
    holiday heroin gave me was dreamscapingly gun-smitten,
but I want to come home. How much guts it takes to bite down on that
    inevitable drill. I want to go down
and you will enter the phase in which no one initiates your bloodstream to come
    up besides this fuck-up. Let me
trouble you more. I bring the things you most enjoy, and we picnic on the bed of
    our settling into the brave new sense of time, like unclucking insomniacs.

Get the red pen out, darling. I never said I could perfect any of it. I opened my
    mouth to speak when I was speechless at fourteen
and wished only that you existed. Piece yourself, uncannily. I need all of you in my
    wound and when the healing begins the future flashbacks will corroborate
finally finding hope. And what pain. And what destruction. Erasure of the time
    that wanted to hurt. I'll peel it back
suck on it with my new clean idiom.
                                  Be in your new limbs from Sunday, I come
    back hungrier, and suck; venom
I spit down the drain. Nothing turns black. The day turns on our faltering spindle;
    a cure, and nocturnal we unwrap the most precious wanted thing; powderless.
Substance in the form of sibling *wow* and a lick worthy of rapture. Oh I applaud
    what you've done to me. Sweetheart, I
live. Consciousness will rave with or without us; be in it and consent to riding it –
    ally, and zero dark.

NEVER TO BE EXTINGUISHED FLAME

The "many chambered heart" of Lorna Goodison

Dzifa Benson

Lorna Goodison's poetry is something of a wily creature. It resists wrangling into one thing or the other, refuses to be leashed to categorisation. Yes, of course, her poetry is a historical, lyrical, linguistic and mythical mapping of Jamaica, rooted in an intimate connection to the land and its people. In that way, it can be classed as a very specific poetry of a very specific place – the poet herself says that she "writes the way Jamaican people tell stories".

This year, Goodison's seventieth, is a momentous one for the poet. Not only has it seen the publication of her *Collected Poems*, it is also the year in which she was appointed Poet Laureate of Jamaica, succeeding Mervyn Morris; she is the first woman to be given such an accolade. It is therefore an opportune time to contemplate the significant contribution she has made to global poetry. Pursuing this quest, I met Goodison during the London launch of the *Collected Poems* this summer and continued the conversation by email over the following months.

In an oeuvre that spans four prolific decades, starting with the somewhat

Lorna Goodison

ragged and epigrammatic style that characterised the early poems with uneven tempos through to the confidently distilled formal sequences and experimentation of more recent work, Goodison's poetry has always been marked by an unselfconscious and compassionate tilt, indicative of a warm and enquiring (in person she has a contagiously girlish laugh), generous and sensuous poetic personality. This makes for poetry that is not only deeply personal but also incantatory in its universality.

"This is what literature does," says Goodison. "There is a poem named 'Epic' that I first encountered in a book titled *The Banker and the Blackfoot* by J. Edward Chamberlin, who happens to be my husband. It is by the great Irish poet Patrick Kavanagh, and in the last three lines he states: 'Till Homer's ghost came whispering to my mind. / He said: I made the Iliad from such / A local row [...]'". Goodison, with "this many chambered heart", sets out her stall of intentions in the very first poem of her *Collected Poems*, 'I Shall Light a Candle of Understanding...'. It begins with an epigraph in the form of a quotation from Esdras, an apocryphal book of the Bible:

> By the hand that lit the candle.
> By the never to be extinguished flame.
> By the candle-wax which wind-worried drips
> into candle wings luminous and rare.
> By the illumination of that candle
> exit, death and fear and doubt
> here love and possibility
> within a lit heart, shining out.

It's a ventriloquist's act that Goodison performs, using this luminosity to animate the vivid personalities in her family such as her great-grandmother Leanna the Guinea woman, her Amerindian father Marcus whom "wind and string instruments obeyed" ('This is My Father's Country') and her English great-grandfather William Harvey, who gave his name to the river running through the land where he established a homestead. In a mixture of standard English and Jamaican patois, these freewheeling tones and voices accommodate everyone and everything, from the prosaic to the metaphysical, to recount a poetic history of Jamaica that includes the legacy of slavery and sugar plantations, the poverty and illiteracy. They range beyond the poet's homeland too, in keenly observed and protean conversations with artists such as Max Ernst, Vincent Van Gogh, El Greco and Cézanne – which is not surprising given that Goodison paints the cover artwork for her books, including this one, and initially thought that she might become a painter. She told me, "I was not always sure that I wanted to be a poet and thought I would spend my life as a painter who wrote poems on the side. I started out doing both things simultaneously. Obviously, poetry had other ideas for its role in my life. I regret ever having said poetry was a dominating tyrant and hereby apologise to poetry, my faithful friend. Still, I do become very emotional whenever I walk into a painter's studio and smell linseed oil and turpentine."

Other historical figures, such as Rosa Parks, Paul Robeson and Christopher Columbus feature too. Even James Bond, with the swagger of a Jamaican fisherman, makes an appearance. Inevitably, many poets have walk-on parts – Keats, Akhmatova, Wordsworth, Donne, Dante and Walcott, who was a good friend and mentor. In the poem 'Country, Sligoville', a reworking of Yeats's 'Lake Isle of Innisfree', one of the poet's personas takes a walk with Yeats to Sligoville in the Jamaican countryside, "in the shamrock green hills of St. Catherine":

> We swap duppy stories, dark night doings.
> I show him the link of a rolling calf's chain
> and an old hige's salt skin carcass.
>
> Love descended from thickets of stars
> to light Yeats's late years with dreamings
> alone I record the mermaid's soft keenings.

This alignment of Irish and Jamaican lore – the tumultuous histories both cultures share, their intertwined colonial history, the love both poets have for their native countryside (consider how Yeats is informally addressed, how place names echo each other, Jamaican hills become "shamrock green") – is not a coincidence. One of Goodison's grandfathers, George O'Brian Wilson, was an Irishman who married a Guinea woman, Leanna Sinclair, soon after arriving in Jamaica in the mid-1800s. Sligoville was also the first free village and came to embody Jamaican independence. Goodison is also, of course, alluding to County Sligo in Ireland. The poem originally appeared in *Turn Thanks* (1999), a collection that saw Goodison's poetry becoming more introspective than in previous collections, through the new intensity in her writing about family. Ultimately, 'Country,

Sligoville' is a poem about yearning for the connection of kinship, echoed in Goodison's response when I ask her how poetry has changed her:

"I grew up in a big family. It taught me to value solitude. I grew up in the city of Kingston. It taught me to love the countryside. I used to make elaborate plans for my life. None of those plans ever came to fruition. One day I realised that there was another plan at work in my life, one over which I have absolutely no control. All these things I found out through writing my poetry. It taught me much about the reconciliation of opposites."

The poet and novelist Kei Miller writes that Goodison is "a poet who is Metaphysical, Romantic and Postcolonial all at once". Everything does seem to be grist to Goodison's creative mill. Simple things such as washing clothes, a coir mattress or eating a mango (which is also about the act of writing poetry) are invested with the heightened sensibilities of ritual, the veneration usually reserved for religion. More extraordinary events are written as if they are all part of the same fabric. Goodison, then, might be a Jamaican poet but her outlook about what poetry can be is cosmopolitan and inclusive. It's an attitude that was inculcated in her when she was very young and reading authors like Somerset Maugham.

"I am the eighth of nine children and our house was filled with people coming and going all the time. We read a lot of newspapers like Jamaica's *Daily Gleaner*, the British *Daily Mirror*, the *New York Times* and publications like *Time* magazine, brought home by my eldest sister who is now one of the best-known journalists in the Caribbean. I developed the habit of reading widely and eclectically from an early age and my first real job was as a trainee bookmobile librarian. I saw a lot of rural Jamaica through the windows of that enormous green vehicle packed with books we distributed to children in remote parts of the island. Also, my mother relied on her Anglican hymn book and the King James Bible to get her through difficult days, so I grew up seeing someone drawing sustenance from words in books."

The mother figure in Goodison's poetry isn't restricted to her own mother, Doris (although the poems that do focus on her are some of her most popular, among them 'I Am Becoming My Mother', 'My Mother's Sea Chanty' and 'After the Green Gown of My Mother Gone Down'), or even her mother's mother and her great-grandmother – such familial poems are a rich seam running throughout the book. She also explores the role of woman as both creator and destroyer. Goodison maintains, "The world is in need of mothering. Good mothers are anxious that their children should not go hungry. They strive to strengthen and protect the weak and the vulnerable. They want a bright future for their children. We need more of that good mothering from our leaders. I am very taken with John Keats's belief that the world is a vale of soul making, and mothering is essential to soul making, I am thinking these days of the role of the divine mother in the scheme of things."

The divine mother is a theme that Goodison has addressed many times, as here in the first stanza of 'Mother, the Great Stones Got to Move':

> Mother, one stone is wedged across the hole in our history
> and sealed with blood wax.
> In this hole is our side of the story, exact figures,
> headcounts, burial artifacts, documents, lists, maps
> showing our way up through the stars; lockets of brass
> containing all textures of hair clippings.
> It is the half that has never been told,
> and some of us must tell it.

There are many kinds of women here. They are matriarchs, tightrope walkers, lepidopterists, mermaids, proprietresses, spinsters, puppeteers, lovers, warriors and yes, poets too. They are objects of desire, abuse and worship. They include wild, defiant, mad, corpulent, poor, mysterious, nameless women who can be drunk in the morning, with eyes that glow like coals and smiles like wet moonstone. Old women in the poem 'Where I Come From' "bind living words / across their flat chests so their flesh becomes legacy and memory for the future". Often, it seems the poet is in conversation with herself, adopting personas that recur and admonish in poems such as 'Mulatta Song', 'Mulatta Song II', 'The Mulatta as Penelope' and 'Mulatta and the Minotaur', which reference Homer. The cumulative effect of all this is to give the reader the uncanny sensation of listening in on the poet's private thoughts. We also encounter the likes of Winnie Mandela and Billie Holiday, for example in 'A Small Blues for Lady's Gardenia'. These days Goodison's regard for the stories of women extends to the obligations she has taken on as Poet Laureate of Jamaica. In partnership with the National Library of Jamaica (who also administer the laureateship), Goodison spearheads a programme called 'All Flowers Are Roses: Poetry and Self-Defence', which combines lessons in self-defence with poetry workshops to foster confidence and self-esteem in young girls from inner-city Kingston.

The spectres of colonialism and slavery and their attendant difficult legacies inevitably rear their heads in the *Collected Poems*. This is most apparent in the poems harvested for this volume from Goodison's seventh collection *Travelling Mercies* (2001). It isn't that poems dealing with these themes are absent from earlier poems. Rather, poems such as 'Book' – a searing indictment of the cost of slavery through the figure of Quashie – written during this period, coincide with the increasing prowess of a poet who has paid her dues, who is confident in her ability to hold and shape a more formal line while allowing herself the freedom to experiment with length, abstractions and the density of mysticism and allusion. But there is no posturing here, no will to bamboozle the reader with oblique references in the transmuting of other people's stories. Goodison treads lightly among these dark themes and in so doing neatly sidesteps polemics, but the poems still have the bite that signals anger layered onto what is left unsaid. Here's 'Reporting Back to Queen Isabella', for instance:

When Don Cristobal returned to a hero's welcome,
his caravels corked with treasures of the New World,
he presented his findings; told of his great adventures
to Queen Isabella, whose speech set the gold standard
for her nation's language. When he came to Xamaica
he described it so: 'The fairest isle that eyes ever beheld.'
Then he balled up a big sheet of parchment, unclenched,
and let it fall off a flat surface before it landed at her feet.
There we were, massifs, high mountain ranges, expansive
plains, deep valleys, one he'd christened for the Queen
of Spain. Overabundance of wood, over one hundred
rivers, food, and fat pastures for Spanish horses, men,
and cattle; and yes, your majesty, there were some people.

Goodison says, "I have always found great wisdom in this quotation by W.B. Yeats: 'Out of the quarrel with others we make rhetoric; out of the quarrel with ourselves we make poetry.' I wanted my voice to reflect more of the quarrel with myself, so I tried very hard not to let that rhetorical voice rule my poetry. I think that approach came about because I was politically active in Jamaica during the 1970s and I attended and participated in countless anti-apartheid and anti-imperialist rallies where

I heard many protest poems. Perhaps my most successful 'protest' poem is 'Bedspread', written for Winnie Mandela. It was inspired by an incident that occurred during apartheid when the South African police raided her home and seized a bedspread because it was in the colours of the ANC. The tone of that poem is anything but rhetorical, but it still got the anti-apartheid message across. I had the honour of reading it to her in person when the Mandelas visited Jamaica in 1994."

Much is made of the numinous qualities of Goodison's poetry, exemplified in the leitmotif of light. But there is another thematic preoccupation that flies somewhat under the radar. It takes immersion in a volume as expansive as this *Collected Poems* for that to become apparent. If the theme of light allows the poems to occupy transcendental realms, then salt tethers them to much that is terrestrial and tangible. It's "where salt agrees with sweet flesh". Salt appears as a captor – "Loose now / the salt cords / binding our tongues / splitting our palettes / causing us to speak blood" ('Songs of Release') – and lover:

> Would that mean that salt
> would be savoring through our honey?
> And you say, "What of
> it?" and give me a kiss
>
> flavoured with honey and sea-salt mix.
> ('Aunt Rose's Honey Advice')

It's the stuff of no-good men – "True I returned from the quayside / my eyes full of sand / and his salt leaving smell / fresh on my hands" ('Mulatta as Penelope') – and protection against those who would do harm: "When you dwell among enemies / you never make them salt your pot. / You never make them know / your want" ('Thyme'). Elsewhere it symbolises healing, ritual, seasoning, legacy, preservative, covenant... not forgetting that "hige's salt skin carcass" in Sligoville. In addition salt is sucked by slaves while other people crave it. The sea has a particular shade of salt that colours its foam and there's even a poem called 'Island of Salt'. In the poem 'Guernica', the poet writing about Manhattan alludes to Lot's wife admitting: "I confess. I looked behind as I left."

There are also a remarkable number of poems with the word "song" in their title or in the body of a poem. Is music the beating heart of

Goodison's poetry? There's good argument for this even in the "many chambered heart" of the *Collected Poems*. The book is peopled with music personalities such as Keith Jarrett, Charles Mingus and Jimmy Cliff and is full of ska, rocksteady and reggae cadences and rhythms. I imagine Goodison composing her poems to a soundtrack.

"I believe there may be a soundtrack that accompanies my writing process," Goodison agrees. "It's hard-wired into me, I grew up in a household where everybody loved music. My father could play the guitar and my mother could pick out hymns on a piano. Several of my siblings are involved in the Jamaican music industry and I believe that my own poetic voice rests on a foundation of melodies and rhythms I absorbed from hymns and popular songs I heard as a child. I also heard a lot of jazz and rhythm and blues played by my brothers. I fell in love with Miles Davis's music when at age ten I heard a recording of 'Kinda Blue'. I named my son Miles, that's how much I love Miles Davis."

When *Collected Poems* was published earlier this summer, the London launch at Waterstones bookshop on Gower Street was attended by high-profile Caribbean writers such as Kei Miller, Malika Booker and Linton Kwesi Johnson, more accustomed to being on stage than in the audience, as well as acclaimed artists and academics of every hue. This is, I believe, further testament to how much Goodison and her poetry are beloved. This book – more accurately described as a tome, such is its size – rather than overwhelming the reader, makes it clear how wide-ranging Goodison's poetry is and illustrates the sheer magnitude of her contribution to the canon of global poetry in English. The book distils Goodison's core poetic subjects over forty years and ten poetry collections, and that's discounting the three short-story collections, the celebrated memoir and the paintings. Her exuberant poetry has a physicality to it that is visceral and immediate. It's poetry as embodied practice, not poetry as intellectual hijinks.

I ask a final question: "Are you a philosopher and a historian moonlighting as a poet?"

"I hope so!" Goodison says.

Lorna Goodison, Collected Poems, Carcanet, £14.99,
ISBN 9781784104665

Report

THE HOUSE OF PAIN AND MENDING

On Prison Poetry

Kate Potts

This year The Koestler Trust, a prison arts charity which encourages people within the criminal justice system to engage in the creative arts, published *Koestler Voices*, the first of a new biannual anthology of poetry from prisons. As editor, I drew together a selection of poems from the winners of the 2016 and 2017 Koestler Awards for poetry. The entries were fantastically various: hand-scrawled, printed, or typed out and painstakingly fastened into handmade booklets; humorous, passionate, political, wry, allegorical, intimate, moving. These were artefacts, dispatches from a strange, seemingly distant world which most of the population will never experience first-hand.

The link between poetry and incarceration is a well-worn one. Poetry continues, in the twenty-first century, to be associated with ideas of imaginative freedom, truth-telling, and voicing the unspoken or unspeakable. Its rootedness in oral traditions and its concentrated, image-rich and often rhythmic nature make it an apt means of representing and preserving memory, of bearing witness. Poetry can be composed with even the sparest of materials: scraps of paper, a fingernail and a brick wall, the lines you rehearse and recite inside your head. The potential political power of the poet's blank page is so great that governments continue to imprison poets – Eritrean poet Amanuel Asrat and Palestinian poet and photographer Dareen Tatour, to give just two recent examples – for writing-related activities. But there's also a long history of people entering prison for reasons not directly related to writing, and producing work inspired, necessitated, and even facilitated by life inside. Oscar Wilde wrote 'The Ballad of Reading Gaol' (1898) after serving his sentence for "gross indecency". Etheridge Knight's debut collection *Poems from Prison* (1968) was written during an eight-year stretch for armed robbery. "I died in 1960 from a prison sentence," he said, "and poetry brought me back to life."

Koestler Voices is one of many English-language anthologies of contemporary prison writing, though relatively few of these are solely dedicated to poetry. UK prison magazine *Inside Time* has produced two anthologies showcasing the poems submitted to its poetry page. The PEN America anthology *Doing Time: 25 Years of Prison Writing* (1999) is perhaps the closest, in terms of breadth and variety, to the Koestler anthology project. These anthologies are, of course, fundamentally different to the average poetry anthology. They come into existence for a complex set of reasons: to draw attention to the work of the charities that produce them; to provide insights into life inside the closed world of the prison system and into the broader lives of the people who exist inside it; to make possible, and to underline the importance of, creative communication and expression for everyone – including, controversially, people whose crimes may seem abhorrent and difficult to comprehend. These poems, produced with the support of classes, workshops and mentoring, or entirely independently, are 'prison poetry'. They emerge from within a community that's purposefully and systematically set apart, stigmatised, and detached from the everyday routines and preoccupations of the general population.

Then Home Secretary Michael Howard controversially declared in 1993 that "Prison works" – as a deterrent and a means of protecting the public from crime. Prison has also, from the eighteenth century onwards, been intended as a space for rehabilitation that will lead to positive change in prisoners' lives and reduce reoffending rates. In the past few decades the prison population in England and Wales has more than doubled, rising from 41,561 in 1993 to 86,256 in 2017 according to government figures. In terms of demographics, the UK prison population provides a sort of skewed, exaggerated map of disadvantage: all the usual markers of deprivation – and indicators of discrimination – are overrepresented in the prison population. A 2002 government report found that 23% of the UK prison population had been in care during childhood, 29% had suffered childhood abuse, 46% came from a home where they'd experienced or witnessed violence, 15% were homeless directly before going to prison, 62% had drug problems, and 90% showed signs of a mental health problem. Around 25% of the UK prison population is from a minority ethnic group, compared with 10% of the general population. Among prisoners under eighteen, this rises to 40%. A 2016 government report headed by MP David Lammy found that black, Asian and minority ethnic people are more likely to be sentenced to prison for some crimes, such as driving, public order, and drug offences, and are likely to be given longer sentences for these crimes than those who are white. Prison conditions in England and Wales have been in the news in recent years, with reports of widespread drug use, overcrowding and riots. There are concerns over the drastic cuts to the prison and probation service budget in recent years. The government's safety in custody bulletin shows that in the year to March 2017 incidents of self-harm, assaults on fellow prisoners, and assaults on prison staff reached record highs. In this context creative work that emerges from, responds to, and examines our prison system seems more vital than ever.

There's a great deal we don't know about the poets featured in *Koestler Voices*, many of whom remain anonymous through choice or necessity, but we do know that they are all, or have previously been, detained within the UK's criminal justice system. Like 'outsider art', prison poetry may be self-taught, and partially removed from the production and publishing networks that exist in the wider world. These poems often display a disregard for literary fashion and convention, as well as conventions of punctuation and grammar. When I (lightly) edited them, I tried hard to differentiate between conscious creative decisions and decisions made – or avoided – through lack of formal learning. The poems demonstrate a strong preoccupation with the aspects of life that prison tightly controls: time and space. They are also engaged in finding the means to figuratively break out of or rise above incarceration, to "get out of the state of mind of being in prison" as Stuart, one of the poets featured in *Koestler Voices*, puts it. These poets write to regain power, often through chronicling and critique, or imaginative transcendence or escape. As editor Bell Gale

Chevigny observes in *Doing Time*, "Coming to terms with time" is something poets tend to be familiar with: "Poets know time's brevity, its repeats and deceits, and also how rhythm mimics time, how imagination cheats it."

Wilde's 'The Ballad of Reading Gaol', with its mournful, rhythmic repetitions and solemn lament 'breaks out' of the speaker's powerlessness by chronicling and critiquing prison conditions and the justice system, and appealing for readers to acknowledge the complexity and common humanity of prisoners. In a similar way, many of the poems in *Koestler Voices* both respond to the concept of prison and function as testimony to the poet's individual experience inside it. 'Dirty Laundry' presents a playful, relatively positive vision of the rehabilitation and redemption prison narrative, with time in prison working as a sort of automatic wash cycle that achieves "a cleansing of hearts". 'IF' updates Kipling's hymn to a particular kind of British, colonial masculinity into a guide to surviving prison: "If you can sleep in bed while tannoys beckon / A long and seemingly endless list of names". In 'Networked Gym-Fit Recidivist' a confident, confiding narrator offers a list-form exposé of prison life which is explicitly designed for an outside audience, ultimately concluding, in contrast to 'Dirty Laundry', that the prison system is "just a scam":

> I've learnt a broken-legged Vietnamese was
> > untreated for sixteen days.
> I've learnt a man from Vilnius
> > pulled out four of his own teeth.
>
> [...]
>
> I've learnt that despite private profit's prison glass
> > there's neither rehabilitation nor correction
> > > with many street-homeless post-detention.

'A is for...' constructs a discussion of the idea and means of incarceration, this time through a stark, capitalised A to Z listing that juxtaposes Attica with Auschwitz, Folsom with Guantanamo Bay and, finally: "X-RAY / YAMAGUCHI / Z-CAMP / ZYKLON B".

While these poems find their power in recording, commenting on or critiquing the prison experience, a number of the poems in *Koestler Voices* avoid confinement figuratively through identification with the world outside, and through discussion of artistic transcendence. In 'The Piano Player' there's an idea of transcendence and consolation through music:

> the piano player
> strolled sex
> over ebony and ivory
> his fingers knew
> highs and lows
> of down and out days
> when sound
> was all there was
> between
> lust and loneliness

In 'Skein', there's transcendence in the birds' freedom of movement, mirroring the formal and imaginative freedom of the poem itself. The poem traverses the page in the chevroned 'V' shape of geese in flight. Unlike the speaker, the birds

> NEED NO RELEASE
>   TO FLEE THE CHILL
>   WINTER DARK
>   FREEZING NIGHTS

The geese's migration, nesting, and raising of their young contrasts with the speaker, whose centred, static viewpoint is contained in the lines at the sharp base of the 'V', the same lines that anchor the 'V' shape in the page's crease: "coz I will still / be watching here", "but I will still / be watching here". The speaker is distant from many of the cycles of the natural world, but nevertheless feels connected to them through observation. This desire for communion with wildness and the non-human world – intensified by the prison's relative detachment from nature – recurs in 'Whales' ("From my cell window / I see the long curves of the Downs / Like great whales") and in 'Sonnet for a Cretan Tree'.

'Eviction Day' uses the outside world, rather than prison, as a space for social and political critique. The poem lists discarded belongings, building a picture of a lost home:

A pair of rain-wearied Nikes
A pink soft toy, muddied
A teething ring

[...]

Take only what you can carry
Pack the year into boxes
The bailiff's appointment is fixed.

The poem invokes the housing crisis without veering away from the central, human story of a single eviction. The lines "We're all Rachman's children now" and "We're all Hoogstraten's children now" recall the crimes of Britain's most notorious slum landlords. 'Never Again?' uses quotes from the news media as the starting point for a commentary on issues around migration, extrapolating from and pulling apart the language of bureaucratic authority, its euphemistic double-speak in particular:

[...] and we drag children from trailer containers
To hold them in freight sheds
While fat white men who hold money overseas
Talk of 'one in, one out' and 'fast-track returns'

A number of poems depict authoritarian dystopias ('See nothing, hear nothing, speak nothing', 'Thirteen-O-Clock'), as well as new takes on folk tales, fairy tales and fables. Perhaps the most successful of these is 'The Sun Did Not Rise', in which the people's response to the surreal absence of the sun is curiously muted and habitual. It's the habit, blind hope and persistence of the poem's "we" in the face of catastrophe that rings true in a peculiarly British way. The images are both fairy-tale clichéd and wonderfully strange: the rain falls "like tears from heaven", the sun "cannot abandon you at night". In the end, the narrator offers an understated vision of solidarity and comfort:

A stranger turned to me and whispered,
'If our hearts are warm, will that not do?'
I thought for a moment and replied,
'Perhaps we just need to stand closer together.'

The absent sun isn't presented as a metaphor, though its strangeness invites this kind of interpretation: it's enough that the sun is a fundamental part of the natural world, the source of heat, warmth, light, energy and nourishment. The imagery in this poem is strikingly similar to Etheridge Knight's prison poem 'The Sun Came', in which the coming of the sun is the coming of truth or enlightenment – in this case related to the coming of the civil rights activist Malcolm X – which is at first squandered or poorly handled. But in 'The Sun Did Not Rise' there's no such idea of the potential for enlightenment or radical change. There is, though, a sense of quiet solidarity in the face of disaster.

The poems in *Koestler Voices* that describe life outside work to capture, chronicle and valorise particular experience, including experience of life on the margins, and cultures traditionally underrepresented in poetry for the page. There are a few poems that skilfully, often humorously, use Scottish vernacular language: 'The Visit Hall Beckons', 'Killie Bus Tales', 'Dys-Leg-Sarah' and 'Glesga Jesus': "I wance met Jesus in Glesga, / Hunkered in a doorway, doon the west end / Can o'Carlsberg in his haun."

The voices in these poems are strong and acutely observed, recalling use of the vernacular voice in African-American prison and protest poetry. The precision the poems in the anthology utilise in their descriptions of life outside might be, in part, a reflection of the relative monotony of prison life. As Clare Fisher, who teaches creative writing in prisons, explains: "Simple things such as watching strangers play football in a park [...] become opportunities for wonder and awe."

Another way in which prison poetry might 'work' is as a safe space that facilitates deep contemplation, a working through of what's difficult to communicate or express, the development of new perspectives, and movement towards a kind of rehabilitation of the self. In 'The House of Pain and Mending' unspoken memory and emotion is experienced physically and viscerally, through the body and the environment, the pile-up of verbs suggesting a silent crescendo of pain:

In the house of pain and mending
furniture and fabrics hiss and groan
with secret hurts whispered pummelled
yelled communicated through the skin.

Many poems are addressed, often intimately, to particular unnamed interlocutors, in a manner that emphasises and plays on the peculiar estrangement of prison life but also, in poems such as 'Grandfather Clock', works through the history of past relationships to come to some sort of accommodation and acceptance. Like 'The House of Pain and Mending', 'Grandfather Clock' depicts memory and emotion as constrained, held in:

> You kept my heart under a stone brother,
> almost like it meant something.
> A thousand tiny fireflies in a jar brother,
> unquiet spirits
> on the tangled path from childhood.

This is a poem that juxtaposes toughness ("I'll fight you for the grandfather clock / that stood sentry through our sleepless nights") with emotional vulnerability. The poem also demands that the addressee, the "brother" (and we, as readers) share intimately in this experience of the past. The poem becomes a means of self-recognition and, at the same time, a space for connection and mutual recognition with others.

Angela Davis, speaking about the US prison system, suggests that prison can be a form of escape and avoidance for the un-incarcerated: "It relieves us of the responsibility of seriously engaging with the problems of our society, especially those produced by racism and, increasingly, global capitalism." As with all the poems in this anthology, 'Grandfather Clock' underlines prisoners' complexity, diversity and humanity, and their status as citizens despite their crimes and their confinement. Discussing his curation of the Koestler 2017 art exhibition *Inside*, the artist Antony Gormley emphasised the value and importance of prisoners' perspectives, proposing that "if astronauts were the great explorers of the twentieth century, perhaps prisoners can be the psychonauts of the twenty-first". He acknowledged the art of prisoners as "an amazing kind of vindication of the human spirit under extreme circumstances". Through their accommodation with the constraints of poetic form, of language itself, and of everyday prison life, these poems engage with ideas and experiences of imprisonment that are relevant well beyond the prison walls.

Koestler Voices: New Poetry from Prisons, vol. 1, *ed. Kate Potts,*
with a foreword by Benjamin Zephaniah, The Koestler Trust, £10,
ISBN 9780957410183

ARRIVALS

Ten: Poets of the New Generation, *ed. Karen McCarthy Woolf,*
Bloodaxe, £9.95, ISBN 9781780373829

Bidisha celebrates a new anthology of emerging poets

. . .

T en: *Poets of the New Generation* is a box of delights, a quick and
inspiring flash through the work of ten emergent British poets,
introduced briefly by the ten rather more established poets who have been
matched with them through the Complete Works mentoring scheme,
including Pascale Petit and Liz Berry.

The Complete Works was established a decade ago by the writer
Bernardine Evaristo to counteract publishing's underrepresentation of
British Asian and Black British poets and to diversify the poetry scene.
The scheme has produced two prior anthologies in 2010 and 2014 (also
published by Bloodaxe) and has been a huge success, driving change
within the industry and transforming shortlists for the major prizes. To
give some indication of the Complete Works' acuity in picking out great
talent, the scheme's previous 'fellows' include Sarah Howe, Malika Booker
and Mona Arshi.

This third anthology gives the reader the sensation of moving quickly
through a brightly chattering crowd in which observation, reaction and
interpretation, along with subject matter both light and dark, doggedly

personal and expansively wide-ranging, terse and voluble, mix easily together. As the anthology's editor and former Complete Works fellow, poet Karen McCarthy Woolf, writes in her introduction, "amongst the group all five continents are represented and consequently so too, moments of linguistic and cultural hyphenation and hybridity". Of course there are some writers included here who are still very much at the beginning of a journey to find a distinctive voice, form and subject matter. Nonetheless, there are several standout talents.

The collection opens with the powerful, novelistic and versatile work of Omikemi Natacha Bryan. In 'While She Waits for a Heart to Arrive (a Prayer)' hidden traumas try to emerge from "a backroom". In this breathless, splintery poem memories of violent incidents recur in unspeakable flashes so that the story "burns [...] falls apart / in my mouth." Yet speaking provides no release as it cannot stop trauma: "stop / I said / but he kept going / & the brother / on the bottom bunk / heard nothing." In the poem 'Crownsville', set in a hospital which was once the site of unethical medical experiments against African-American children, the stanzas are solid and square, flowing smoothly with close details narrated by a wistful inmate: "I haven't seen kin / since the last light we had was snow." Bryan excels when her forms cohere and she marries serious, prosy observation with terrible foreboding, as in her description of a sinister old woman with hair like "a shock / a wish blown through a dandelion clock" ('The Warner'). I have no doubt that she will soon become a major and deeply serious voice in world literature.

By contrast, Anglo-Indonesian writer Will Harris brings sardonic levity. He is wonderfully inventive, with a formal sparseness and a great, flat wit. His poem 'Object' is a deadpan tug of words between opposing parties, be they lovers, diplomats from warring countries or competing gamblers: "What have you taken?" says one. The other replies, "What you have taken." Finally the first speaker concludes, "I have taken nothing from you." The enemy replies, "Then I have taken nothing." This equivocal, ambiguous end – neither a concession nor a retreat, neither a rapprochement nor an admission – characterises all Harris's poems here. Visiting Jakarta in 'Mother's Country', he does not hail any great homecoming, instead saying that "After years of [...] holding back, / I have no more excuses." His words fall lightly on the page but leave a wry smile long after.

Poet, essayist and co-editor of digital platform Diaspora Drama, Momtaza Mehri has already rightfully garnered much praise for her work.

She has been shortlisted for the Brunel African Poetry Prize and will be having her chapbook *sugah.lump.prayer* published as part of the New Generation African Poets series. Just as her characters cross continents between America, Africa and Europe, her lines drip across the page and then pull back sharply, stagger down into lists and tighten into blocky paragraphs. Yet her language has a contrasting steadiness and maturity, with a lovely sense of pace. In her poem 'I believe in the transformative power of cocoa butter and breakfast cereal in the afternoon' she evokes a luxurious sense of ease and distance in which people "drink from time's cup" and the breeze is at once loving and aggravating, "like an aunt, tugging at our scalps". Mehri's pliancy with language and image is so sure, so wise: life itself is a "bottled sigh" in that first poem, while in another work, '<p>Grief in HTML</p>', the afterlife is described as "a quasi-dream". Both evoke a sense of poignancy, cosily contained. I love the contrast between her humorous forms and titles and the generous wisdom within.

Other poets in the collection offer purely sensual pleasures. The vivid work of Buenos Aires-born Londoner Leonardo Boix is so strongly influenced by visual art that his colours and images jump off the page and melt in the mouth. Each poem breaks down into subheadings and numbered sections which roll on exhilaratingly, perfectly formed. Like a box of watercolours, the poem 'Pigments alla prima' contains numerous tiny but exquisite three-line stanzas inspired by the names of paint colours, so 'Lead White' evokes "Mother's body resting / a marble emptiness" while 'Ivory Black' recalls "A scared panther in an Argentine circus". This is poetry of highly subjective, sumptuous vision and sexily sordid tactility in which a dishevelled bedroom by the sea smells of "salt and leathery seaweed" while seagulls "echo down chimneys" and breakfast is cooked "in a dirty pan" ('Ode to Deal'). Boix's sure, sophisticated grasp of the physical world and his easy, positive descriptions feel like an indulgent treat.

Degna Stone's work moved me with its sophisticated, sensitive examination of grief, regret and time. In 'Cross Bones Burial Ground' she picks out the touchingly fragile things ordinary people leave to commemorate the dead: "dried up roses faded to brown, / a handmade, Red Cross flag [...] champagne corks, raffia bows [...] greyed-out red ribbon". She aptly describes the loneliness and brutality of city life, using the image of a major city built around a river to reference themes of homecoming, migration and escape. The characters in her poem 'The River Gods' don't wish to escape anywhere, but have grown cynical about urban living and "don't believe in river gods [...] don't pray". In the twenty-first century, the true icons are buildings and bridges "built in steel" that "span the water like pagan priests". Stone's work examines the survival of humanity amongst these man-made gods.

Finally, Jennifer Lee Tsai is a great find, balancing a certain lightness and sharp observation with a questing, plainspoken sincerity. She uses her imagery delicately and well, with irony. In 'Black Star' she berates a bad boyfriend in a weightless hail of recriminations: he is "everything I hadn't wished for [...] a name I couldn't say / a train journey I shouldn't have gone on [...] a crow crowing over me". And yet the overall atmosphere of her work is one of effortless mobility and freedom, never dragging the reader down. The poems set in Hong Kong are standouts, describing a place where past and present, tourism and heritage, surface aesthetics and deeper meaning merge: trees in a temple courtyard are "strewn with coloured streamers, / fluttering desires" ('The Valley Spirit Never Dies'); when arriving on the island Tsai comments, "This is where my past begins" ('New Territories').

As well as being a literary endeavour, *Ten: Poets of the New Generation* is a form of activism and a show of solidarity in which established voices stand up for and celebrate lesser-known ones. The Complete Works project has changed the literary world measurably, letting in variety not just of race, sex and cultural identity but also of voice, form, attitude, outlook and experience. While the impressive writers I've named here go above and beyond in fleshing out and shoring up those poets in the anthology who have yet to find their groove, it's still a wonderfully accessible showcase for thrilling new talent and, overall, a joy to read.

Bidisha is a writer, filmmaker and broadcaster. Her first film is An Impossible Poison.

APPROPRIATE MEASURES

Thom Gunn, Selected Poems, *ed. Clive Wilmer, Faber, £16.99,*
ISBN 9780571327690

Kit Fan considers the fusion of life and work in this new selection

. . .

Abook of collected poems, posthumous or otherwise, radiates a poet's work against a total horizon, occupying a larger symbolic space than the individual collections. If the 'collected' suggests a solar, monumental completeness, a 'selected' seems a lunar counterpart – less definable, more like images reflected from a larger body, and by its selective nature, counter-definitive. Gunn edited seven selections of other poets, most notably Fulke Greville, Ben Johnson, Ezra Pound, and Yvor Winters – all of whom influenced him deeply. He also compiled three Faber selecteds from his own work; the most iconic, in 1962, co-starred Ted Hughes – a book touched by the hands of many A-level students. All three appeared before his *Collected Poems* in 1994, his last book *Boss Cupid* in 2000, and his sudden death in 2004. Posthumous selected poems, often done by a fellow poet or admirer, are an important and difficult genre. If death provides finality to a poet's career, it also enables new kinds of visibility and freedom of interpretation. In this vein came August Kleinzahler's *Selected Poems of Thom Gunn* (2009) published by FSG in the US, showcasing a formally stylish and eclectic Gunn. Clive Wilmer's informative and carefully annotated book is more interested in representing the arc of Gunn's career as it relates to his life, framing his work through illuminating biographical material largely culled from the Bancroft Library Archive at Berkeley where Gunn taught over four decades.

Biography, interestingly, has sat awkwardly with Gunn throughout his career. In a rare autobiographical piece, 'My Life Up to Now', from his selected essays, *The Occasions of Poetry* (1982), Gunn wrote that "the danger of biography, and equally of autobiography, is that it can muddy poetry by confusing it with its sources". 'The Gas-poker', a harrowing poem about his mother's suicide and one of the finest elegies of the last century, was published in his last book in 2000. Wilmer's *Selected* includes the detailed account Gunn wrote in his diary after her death in 1944, when he was fifteen. Written in the third person, the poem's emotional intensity is suppressed by Gunn's diffident quietness, translating traumatic experiences into something strangely distanced from the self: "They who had been her treasures / Knew to turn off the gas, / Take the appropriate measures, / Telephone the police."

This reminds us that throughout his career, Gunn wrote against the grain of Confessional poetry. It is as though his poetry depended on him treating himself as someone else, or nobody in particular, someone almost anonymous. Gunn never claimed the Orphic privileges of the 'Poet' or a 'Poet's Life' like Robert Lowell or Sylvia Plath. He was content to operate within the republic of contingency. Wilmer's edition juxtaposes Gunn's poems with these often revealing biographical materials, providing interesting backdrops for Gunn's distancing act.

Wilmer's selection also gives us glimpses of the early Gunn thriving through poses and disguises in *Fighting Terms* (1954) and *The Sense of Movement* (1957), while their cool, sexually coded, and existentialist energies were transformed into a more varied, contradictory, and freer voice in *My Sad Captains* (1961), which reads in many ways like a farewell to his earlier iconographic repertoire. His next book *Touch* (1967) seems a not-quite-achieved prelude to the shape of things to come, groping towards a new idiom born of his encounters with LSD and sexual liberation on the one hand and American verse post William Carlos Williams on the other. Even after his chronicles of gay liberation, Beat culture and hallucinogenic experiments in coming-out books like *Moly* (1971), Gunn appears to have been strangely disenchanted by his own cult of hedonism, as when one of Circe's drugged pigs exclaims in 'Moly': "Oh a man's flesh already is in mine. / Hand and foot poised for risk. Buried in swine."

Gunn's poetry of sexual and imaginative liberation was succeeded by saddened reflections on the vanity as well as the beauty of human wishes. The nightmarish scenarios of *Jack Straw's Castle* (1976) and urban openness in *The Passages of Joy* (1982) give way not only to the beautifully freighted elegies of *The Man with Night Sweats* (1992) but also the disillusioned lyrics from the domain of *Boss Cupid* (2000). Wilmer's edition provides enlightening glimpses of Gunn's half-century career across both sides of the Atlantic, which coincided with increasing tensions within the poetry establishment about the importance of tradition versus individual talent (as ironically captured in 'Expression' when Gunn speaks of the "very poetic poetry" of his juniors), as well as ferocious conflict over identity politics, fought out in terms of race, gender, and sexuality, particularly in the US.

Critics recognised Gunn's seemingly effortless technical elegance, particularly his medium-like ability to resuscitate the style of the high formalist poets of Elizabethan and Jacobean England in his records of gay bars, drugs, AIDS, rock and roll, casual sex, and alternative forms of sociability associated with post-1960s California. Rhythmic control is at the heart of Gunn's poetic imagination, and it is important to remember that the measured experiments of stunning syllabic poems like 'Considering the Snail' enabled him to write mesmerising unfolding free verse in 'Touch' and 'The Artist as an Old Man'. Gunn's formal intelligence returns in *The Man with Night Sweats*, which contains some of the most moving English-language poems of the last century. "Your dying is a difficult enterprise", Gunn begins his equally difficult 'Lament', a poem that gives primacy to a friend dying of AIDS. Told from a first-person perspective, the tightly knitted stanza addresses the second person (the sufferer and "your death"), before moving onto the third person (the comforter and "a friend"). This subtle flow of pronouns constructs an intricate, private web of human connectedness in mourning. Gunn was writing at a time when AIDS elegies proliferated on all fronts, but he turns away from the ceremonies of public mourning and protest typical of the genre, with its hypnotic insistence on consolation. In elegy after elegy, his simple and controlled language refuses large-gestured self-dramatisation, touching instead on the tacit anguish of both the sufferers and witnesses, bringing the whole weight of his sceptical, formal intelligence to bear on the AIDS crisis in San Francisco.

Auden speaks of poetry as "memorable speech", and here is some of Gunn's: "One is always nearer by not keeping still" ('On the Move'); "Resisting, by embracing, nothingness" ('In Santa Maria del Popolo'); "the sniff of the real, that's / what I'd want to get" ('Autobiography'); "I like loud music, bars and boisterous men" ('Transients and Residents'); "My flesh was its own shield: / Where it was gashed, it healed" ('The Man with Night Sweats'); "he fell [...] 'Into the strong arms of Thom Gunn'" ('Duncan'), and "The intellect as powerhouse of love" ('A Wood near Athens'). The numerous memorable phrases in Gunn's poems reveal a poet of masterful contradictions, balancing the personal and the persona, intimacy and promiscuity, vulnerability and defensiveness, risk and trust, love and intellect. Whether or not one agrees with the sentiment, Gunn's assertion of "The intellect as powerhouse of love" demonstrates his continued fidelity to the inspiration of John Donne and the metaphysical poets with whom he identified from the start of his oeuvre, and also to the homoerotic Shakespeare, whose sonnet 'They that have power to hurt and will do none' echoes through 'A Wood near Athens'. Wilmer's edition shows us that Gunn at the end of his career is as traditional a poet (in terms of cadence, stanza, line and form) as at the beginning, but that he has forced traditional poetic forms to respond to contemporary conditions and modern occasions, with an intellectual suppleness and emotional candour that is almost unprecedented, even taking into consideration more overtly experimental poets like Allen Ginsberg or Frank O'Hara. Arguably, this new selection could have given more space to the poems than the notes. Nevertheless, the selection weaves together highlights from Gunn's astonishing career, reminding us that in refusing many of our confident labels about styles and movements and resisting the poetics and politics of 'identity', Gunn has left us a memorable body of work unparalleled among his contemporaries.

Kit Fan's second collection, As Slow as Possible, *is forthcoming from Arc in 2018.*

SQUEEZING BETWEEN THE CORPSES

Pascale Petit, Mama Amazonica, *Bloodaxe*, £9.95,
ISBN 9781780372945
Anne Michaels, All We Saw, *Bloomsbury*, £16.99,
ISBN 9781408880890

Alice Hiller navigates intrauterine universes and secondary surfaces

. . .

Pascale Petit has made a career out of looking where other poets might turn away – and her seventh collection is no exception. *Mama Amazonica* returns to the twinned subjects of her late mother's lifelong mental illness, and the ecology of the Amazon rainforest. Whereas Petit's previous work operates primarily from the poet-daughter's point of view, this time she deliberately enters the consciousness of her "were-mama" ('Jaguar Girl'). 'Jaguar Girl' reveals that the parent who could swim through the "star-splinters / of a mirror" was first admitted to the "kids' asylum" aged nine. 'Serpentarium' refracts the date rape which precipitated her marriage to Petit's father via a hospital art therapy class. A figure of terror and glamour, on the ward the "petals" of her cheeks "spring open" to allow black beetles to "crawl out" ('Mama Amazonica').

To connect with this energy is an act of creative risk as well as courage, requiring Petit's deep imagination to mute temporarily the injuries perpetrated on her by her mother – which her earlier collections record.

The strongest poems here distil an economy of language that shocks and haunts. In 'Miscarriage', Petit's mother has been forced to drink "gin then saffron" by her husband who wants her back at work:

> Afterwards she needs a glass dome
> to lie inside, a red balloon tied to her thigh.
> The doctor calls it the afterbirth
> but she knows it's a balloon
> because she can hear it squeak.

With childish transparency, the mouse-like squeaking of the imagined balloon – calling to mind Albert Lamorisse's 1956 film *The Red Balloon* – places the reader inside a mind that experiences the world other than as it is, and becomes unable to defend itself. The dangers of parenthood for such people are enacted within 'Buck'. The poem finds pregnancy aggressively destructive – the mother "can feel the embryo / hardening like a bullet", and spawns a fawn whose "buds shed velvet / to reveal pistols". Telling us "She gives birth while working / in the brewery heaving crates", 'Buck' also reflects the challenges of conveying such material without overwhelming the overall tone, intermittently an issue throughout *Mama Amazonica*. Many of the poems include direct reportage of mania, psychosis and depression. While this can occasionally dilute the voice by comparison with Petit's previous work, it offers glimpses into closed wards whose patients, like Petit's mother in her lifetime, lack the agency to speak for themselves.

'Fossa' describes "a beast that runs / naked through the streets, / setting fire to bins" and later "races around / their consulting rooms". Here Petit's mother's voice also becomes audible in the memory of how "she sits on the chair / and growls at the ghost / that's always there". In 'Extrapyramidal Side Effects', a fragmented collage of drug therapies and treatments, she "floats in her turquoise negligee / like a manatee in a tank" following the effects of lithium.

The creative gain realised by Petit's temporary surrender of self generates the run of dazzling two-headed poems which conclude *Mama Amazonica*. Recorded with a botanist's accuracy, 'Kapok' figures the top-heavy "queen of the forest" and mother tree, an ecosystem of creaturely life, as "a ladder to climb towards / the leaves of light in their spiral groves". What fells her eventually are the beautiful, daughterly "hanging gardens of orchids"

drinking the rain that filtered softly
through her storeys, like sacramental wine,
their faces lifted to divine moths.

'King Vultures' then reverses this loss and restores Petit's mother to health and life by forfeiting her daughter's existence. Taking the form of a grave ritual played backwards, the poem closes with the vultures still above the poet "as they were / when I lay inside you, my organs shining in the dark / like caskets of jewels to be plundered". Radiant, and viscerally evocative of both the opened body and the silent, intrauterine universe, this image confirms the value of Petit's work of "squeezing between the corpses" ('The Jaguar') in *Mama Amazonica* to make poems that are as radical as they are necessary – because they enable us to see in new ways.

All We Saw, Anne Michaels' fifth collection, derives its energies from intersections. While Petit is primarily a poet of the present moment, Michaels has always been drawn to refractions through time. Working with interwoven repetitions, jump cuts, and multiple ellipses, Michaels' poetry defines its own parameters. Occasionally heavy-handed, her work, like Petit's, is capable of achieving a breathtaking clarity.

Built from six numbered segments, some of which form single, fragmentary sequences, while others are made up of linked poems, *All We Saw* asks what it means to face death, and its aftermath. 'Sea of Lanterns', the opening segment, is spoken in the first person to an unnamed lover, behind whom the reader also stands. Like a twisting Slinky toy, shared memories kaleidoscope in and out of each other in a free-verse unspooling. While the revolving themes of separation and encounter risk eroding the diction into cliché on occasion, the work is repeatedly pulled tight by its specificity of imagery and phrasing, as when the speaker remembers

[...] a room so small
every movement means touching

felled by the rain,
we woke and thought it was night.

This ability to conjure mood has been a feature of Michaels' work from her first collection, *The Weight of Oranges* (1986), which won the Commonwealth Prize, and contributed to the international success of her novel *Fugitive Pieces* (1996). Like reflections in water, 'Sea of Lanterns' closes with a double image, which enacts the twined strands of remembering and mourning, losing and keeping:

> lanterns empty their light
> into the water
> where they are not
> extinguished
>
> each lamp sets fire to the sea,
> igniting where it drowns

Making common ground with art and memory, water here forms a secondary surface. The next sequence of *All We Saw*, titled 'Somewhere Night Is Falling', works with ideas of transmission through fifty-one sentence-vignettes, all beginning with "Somewhere". Spoken by a plural "we", the effect is to widen the focus – "Somewhere a man measures the dimensions of the prison precisely", "Somewhere there is a boy learning to wait". Within these lines, lovers continue to appear and vanish.

The 'Acknowledgements' in *All We Saw* are subtitled "*at the edge of the sea a cairn*" and begin with a list of seven people, including Michaels' mother Rosalind, Mark Strand, and John and Beverly Berger, who died between 2013 and 2017. These losses are felt within the third segment whose poems refer to the approach to and moment of death. While images such as "the joining of souls seaward" ('Black Sea') may not communicate with every reader, Michaels nonetheless arrives at a pared and moving directness, as when she writes in 'Not', "at the end you said: / I want to keep my eyes open, / to miss nothing".

'Bison', which follows, narrates the movement out of life over the course of a single winter's day, with a degree of control and originality that make it one of the strongest pieces in *All We Saw*. Driving to sit with the "you" who is "busy dying", the narrator pauses to watch rocks appear from the mist, and then become living bison. Michaels sets "black earth breathing its winter breath" against the addressee who "dug breath from your lungs" and then, for a moment, "opened your eyes / gripped my hand, your instinctive // joy", only to pass, gradation by gradation, to "the moment desire forcibly / is renamed / grief".

The fifth section offers seven individual poems which seem to respond to the aftermaths of different deaths. Not everything feels grounded, but individual lines and images continue to sing out, leading the reader into the final segment, which gives the book its title. Another fragmented, single poem, this reaches towards an understanding of what joins those now "camouflaged / by immensity", to those who remain. Conflating art with shared memory, the speaker finds

> and where
> you are
> is where you have
> always been,
> looking to the edge of paper   that torn edge
> of sea

Alice Hiller holds a Jerwood/Arvon mentorship and is working on her first collection.

THE TRANSCENDENT FIELD

Harmony Holiday, Hollywood Forever, *Fence, $16.95,*
ISBN 9780986437304
Tyehimba Jess, Olio, *Wave, $25, ISBN 9781940696201*

Dai George considers the expressive and political power
of a hybrid poetics

. . .

These two excellent new books – epic, resourceful, visual, incensed – explode the parameters of modern poetry. Combining prose, lyric, fragments, found text, screenshots, slogans and illustration, they attest to an increasingly vital hybrid poetics evolving on the other side of the Atlantic, in defiance of Trump's zombie white supremacist politics and the subtler exclusions of the liberal establishment. Their overt subject is black musicality, and the parasitic fascination that white culture has with the talented, entertaining, alien other in its midst. Out of this toxic relationship emerges a condition James Baldwin once diagnosed as "schizophrenic", where "to be a Black American is in some ways to be born with the desire to be white". Harmony Holiday excerpts these words opposite a poem titled 'There is this ambivalence that I must deal with', whose speaker wonders "if we're in cahoots with every / oppressor   on every side". In this collusive and painful condition lies a rationale for the hybrid aesthetic, in so far as restless, mutable forms might enact the trauma of a mind divided against itself, caught between assimilation and refusal, patronage and self-determination. Yet paradoxically they might also enable the black voice – or black body – to evade the pigeonholes of a culture that would happily co-opt it. "To enter the transcendent field we started in," declares Holiday in 'for dreamers, for drummers', "you must assimilate those opposites it gazes at, and then you have to testify as them, one by one, alone."

Hollywood Forever, Holiday's second full poetry collection after *Negro League Baseball* (2011), is literally difficult to read. On almost every page the text competes against its backdrop, be that an Ornette Coleman album cover, an Azealia Banks tweet, or a racist poster from the Jim Crow South. These images are as intrinsic to the experience of reading the book as the stark, irregular poems that jut against them. Little effort is made to clarify the font or even to situate it in the foreground, a rebarbative effect that mimics the internet and its hyperreal din. "I couldn't stop googling mugshots," begins 'Recognition Scenes', over a grainy reproduction of Prince staring blankly at the camera. The poem veers catastrophically from allusions to narcotics addiction, domestic servitude and the commodification of black pop music ("these pills / our pills   toppling into sold songs / and mammies on the TV dinner tray in wrong aprons") to the sudden, oblique vision of a lynching ("Mama is no mulatto / casual   swinging from   that oak"). These conflations and accelerations are central to the logic of Holiday's work. A poem will start amid the exploitative junk of the present day, spitting and riffing on what it finds, before a trapdoor opens under it and we're plunged into a nightmare. Again, this effect seems closely linked to the experience of surfing the net. Images proliferate, links are clicked on; historical trauma springs from the subconscious with the speed of a pop-up window.

This is in many respects a hard, unsentimental book, its voice both wary and weary. It testifies, over and again, to "how lonely it is to overcome ourselves and the / choreographed oppression" ('Niggas with wings or a luminous continuity'). But against the grotesque choreography of white racism, Holiday asserts an alternative tradition. A trained dancer, she is steeped in a lineage of black musical futurism running from Billie Holiday and Miles Davis – the latter pictured on the front cover, dazed and bloodied after a beating from a cop – through the cosmic jazz of Sun Ra. She knows how to make language move, and has every right to boast that "my body makes the sentences" ('See how nature can expose a nigga').

Gradually, powerfully – not that it owes anyone this – *Hollywood Forever* works beyond mere anger, "toward a land where the sun kills questions". Its final page contains a photograph of a black woman teaching a young black child how to hold a balletic pose. Like this pose, the work of justice may be complex and arduous, but in Holiday's poetry it moves tantalisingly into focus. The text overlaying the image spells it out: "Reparations begin in the body".

Tyehimba Jess, whose second collection *Olio* recently won a Pulitzer Prize, employs hybrid strategies to less directly confrontational effect. Where Holiday sparks a riot between text and image, challenging her reader to pick out each element against the intrusive noise of the other, Jess curates a signposted gallery where greater emphasis is placed on the traditional lyric virtues of silence and white space. The collection's epigraph defines "olio" first as "a miscellaneous mixture of heterogeneous elements", but then also in a more targeted sense, as "the second part of a minstrel show which featured a variety of performance acts". At a time when hybridity often seems to equate, in itself, to an act of emancipation or resistance, this comes as an uncomfortable reminder that people of colour have long had the variety of their art burlesqued for racist purposes. Jess's *Olio* draws on vaudeville-era language with a historical irony whose queasy frisson can hardly be misunderstood. One sequence has as its header:

ALL COONS LOOK ALIKE TO ME!
A Chant of Merry Coon Song Melodies
GUARANTEED! *ALL TITLES HISTORICALLY ACCURATE!*
GUARANTEED!

This is clever rather than just brutally effective satire, however, because of the way it reaches forward to implicate the modern reader. With their claim that all song titles in the list that follows are "historically accurate", these lines prompt us to examine how easily an enlightened interest in the past can tip over into dangerous appropriation. White people have a deep history of obsessing over, cataloguing and trying to rescue the authenticity of black popular culture, and *Olio* lures one into colluding with that tradition. Replete with appendixes, pullout sections and interviews, it presents its materials with an archivist's meticulous élan.

Jess's difficult task is to recreate the lost voices of real people, born in the Antebellum and Reconstruction South, while honouring their original dignity and autonomy of expression. Broadly he rises to this challenge, establishing a form – the 'syncopated sonnet' – that allows for impressive, polyvocal range. At times the formal inventiveness masks a fairly traditional, even sentimental lyric register, as in 'Millie and Christine McKoy', the opening poem in a sequence about two conjoined twins who were carted around the South as part of a travelling freak show. Admirably, Jess tries to listen for the interior voices of these women, and to explore via the indeterminacy of his form how those voices might have intertwined and answered one another. Their imagined language strikes me as problematically picturesque – Jess relies on phrases such as "our hearts' syncopated tempo" and "we're fused in blood and body – from one thrummed stem" – but the cumulative effect of these performances is persuasive and moving. At the end of the sequence Jess recombines the five McKoy Twins sonnets in a fold-out supplement with the ogling language of the freak show blazoned on the outside flap ("step right up ladies and gents boys and gals and see the two headed nightingale the McKoy Twins"), while inside we find Jess's five original poems arrayed as the points and centre of a 'Syncopated Star'. Far from a gimmick, the novel formatting unlocks a new intensity in the verse, allowing the poems – and, by extension, the sisters – to speak in private, strengthened by solidarity. It's a solution that typifies an ingenious collection, whose author has the grace, the modesty, and the moral imagination to sing in service to the lives of others.

Dai George's first book was The Claims Office *(Seren, 2013).*

TIGHTROPE SONGS

Sinéad Morrissey, On Balance, *Carcanet*, £8.99,
ISBN 9781784103606
Michael Symmons Roberts, Mancunia, *Cape*, £10,
ISBN 9781911214298
JL Williams, After Economy, *Shearsman*, £9.95,
ISBN 9781848615373

Ellen Cranitch on balancing acts, pushing forward and pushing boundaries

. . .

Sinéad Morrissey's exhilarating new collection, *On Balance*, is inspired by things that defy gravity – trapeze artists, feats of engineering, flight. The book encompasses carrier pigeons, aeroplanes and acrobats. What is so gratifying about the volume is just how many of the poems achieve lift-off. Again and again the work delivers a shock of actuality, for it hits you, when a poem attains optimal life. This sixth collection follows *Parallax* which won Morrissey the T.S. Eliot Award in 2014. Reading *On Balance*, you sense a poet supremely liberated, pushing forward in a style that is ever more distinctively her own.

It's Morrissey's innovations with form, her sensitivity to linebreak and white space, that secure the dynamic nature of the work. Form is tested against content, content against form until, as in all the best poems, form is content, there is no division between the two. 'My Life According to You', for example, all breathless gallop and pithy reversal, which recounts a mother's life from a child's perspective, makes use of a skewed line drop to gather voice and move the action forward. The outstanding long poem 'Collier', about the poet's miner grandfather and her grandmother, closes each stanza with words which generate the first line of the following verse. Propulsive, compelling, melding narrative and lyric, Morrissey's poetry combines deep feeling with a probing, philosophical intelligence.

Morrissey's interests are substantial and diverse. They include history, ecology, family and feminism. 'The Mayfly', its light, stepped stanzas washed across four pages, celebrates the 1930s Irish aviator Lilian Bland. In contrast the title poem 'On Balance' is an angry lyric taking on some particularly misogynistic thoughts of Philip Larkin. Yet the collection is profoundly unified as it traces through its different subject areas the central conceit of tension and its metaphorical counterparts; the pull and push of emotion, the claims of different generations, tipping points in ecology, politics, economics, groundedness and flight.

The collection's primary concern, to find the vivid equivalent in language for the weight and release of experience, is consummately achieved in the tour de force which is the first poem, 'The Millihelen' (a millihelen is a fanciful unit of measurement). The poem is set in Belfast, a city Morrissey knows well. The piece conveys the stutter and stateliness of the *Titanic's* launch in one single, meticulously orchestrated sentence. The poem's opening is all elegant stability, the lines slowed by regular pentameter and assonantal vowels, "ladies lining the quay in their layered drapery". But then a blizzard of syntax and agitated meter interrupt the equilibrium to recreate the teetering, cliff-edge moment of the launch: "and it starts / grandstand of iron palace of rivets starts / moving starts slippery-sliding down". This instant of the launch is characterised as a "moment swollen with catgut- / about-to-snap" which pulls the reader up; we know what will ultimately befall this ship. This fascination with, and recasting of, the concept of time is felt again in 'The Singing Gates', which fluidly catches the groundswell of consciousness as thoughts to do with past, present and future converge on a familiar walk.

The separation of poetic self from poetic subject can be fraught, especially when it involves close relations. Striking about Morrissey's work is how sensitively it negotiates this issue. Family members are never reduced to the writer's attitude towards them but freed into the actuality of themselves. The exquisite 'The Rope' locates in the sudden courtesy of two children at play a growing bond that will accompany them through life, "And I can almost see it thicken between you, / your sibling-tetheredness". The piece has the confidence to resolve with the quietest of touches, as the speaker, no longer present in the imagined future, fades from the work. Poems of motherhood are rarely this good.

For all the singular, precisely etched details of a real city – the bulldogs, banks and credit cards, the backyards, bars and washing lines, even the moths and poplars which have darkened as they evolved to survive in the soot of Manchester's industrial past – there's a placelessness to Michael Symmons Roberts's *Mancunia* which indicates that this city is one of the mind. It is a liminal space where past encounters future; death, life; hope, despair; the wished for, what is. It is a world, our world, caught, as Symmons Roberts puts it in 'Self-Portrait with Dog', between "is" and "ought". This question of the gulf between how we should live and how we do, our recurrent failure to make our society more just (the conflicted text, Thomas More's *Utopia*, is one of the inspirations for the collection) is the urgent engine powering the book. These are metaphysical questions and they have always been Symmons Roberts's territory, his past work marked out by them just as much as by its visceral imagery of blood and of the body, evident here again – "the guts, lungs, lights that make us real" ('The Cold').

That there is no easy answer which will heal the chasm between what is and what should be informs the collection's tone: unsettled, wary of pat consolation, the humour often ironic. This is a book of shadows and portents, as in 'My Father's Death' where the speaker anticipates the event – "as if to preview loss might stem its force". The poetry inhabits the public as well as the private sphere, bringing us municipal functionaries as well as the victims of a large metropolis. The excoriating 'In Paradisum' tackles compassion fatigue towards migrants. By making us uncomfortably complicit, it earns its rhetorical stance. Though occasionally some of the poems can feel distanced, when their song does break through it is a moment of illumination, particularly when the lyric voice is buoyed by rhyme – one of the book's chief pleasures is Symmons Roberts's unshowy use of it. 'Tightrope Song' aptly tautens and slackens its rhymed couplets to explore issues of trust and credulity. 'I Shake Out My Coat', which echoes back to the arresting poem 'Pelt' in *Corpus* (2004), speaks volumes about the lives we accrue and the world we have made, in one surreal, symbolic gesture. And in the unrhymed 'Mancunian Misere', the intimate voice and carefully selected present-day detail light up the ancient psalm form as it confesses the speaker's "constancy of inattention" to the natural world and to fellow human beings: "that man-cocoon asleep on the steps / of a new-closed bank where once I queued to find my balance". Symmons Roberts is just as aware as Morrissey of the powerful metaphorical resonance of those last two words.

In her latest book, *After Economy*, JL Williams is interested in pushing the boundaries of language through experiments with syntax, textual signification and sound. She's also concerned with a different kind of threshold, locating some of her poems on the controversial dividing line between 'good' and 'bad' taste. This can result in work that's edgily provocative, such as 'Hey Did You Hear about the Kurds in Turkey?' There are poems on the Brexit referendum, *Breaking Bad* and Slavoj Žižek; Williams's thematic terrain ranges from contemporary politics, culture and theory to the natural world, religion and mythology. 'Bread Song' assaults the visual field through the exhaustive use of the exclamation mark. More potent are the exercises in sonics, such as the liquid beauty of the long vowels which constitute 'Water What Sounds'. The different aesthetics in play make for a rather fractured read and not all the poems crystallise. Sometimes, too, the formal work feels hampered rather than freed by its constraints. However, of the generally strong series of prose-poems, 'While on the plane', about the retrieval of memory in language, stands out. And the final piece 'Bounty', which makes skilful use of lacunae to actualise its questions about life and death, gods and humanity, is striking for its authoritative poise.

Ellen Cranitch's latest collection is The Immortalist *(Templar, 2017).*

Reviews

THE SWIMMING POOL LIBRARY

Elizabeth-Jane Burnett, Swims, *Penned in the Margins*, £9.99,
ISBN 9781908058492
Ágnes Lehóczky, Pool Epitaphs and Other Love Letters, *Boiler House Press*, £7.95, ISBN 9781911343141

Emily Hasler on the poetry of swimming

. . .

These books are not about swimming. In these complex and challenging collections water is not a subject but a medium, and swimming is form rather than theme. In the virtuosic handling of these two poets swimming provides ways of thinking.

Ágnes Lehóczky's *Pool Epitaphs and Other Love Letters* is a sequence, longer than a pamphlet but shorter than a collection – yet it has greater depths then I can hope to chart. Being profoundly self-reflexive, it is its own best description:

> [...] dear dying Author, we
> are looking for an anonymous author who will find, or
> perhaps invent, correlations between swimming pool
> and poem, hieroglyphs and horror, the pale, spectre-
> thin border, the hyper-real *creatura* between pre-
> mortem and posthumous.
>   ('[PE vii; letter VII:13]')

112 The Poetry Review

This is an incredibly intricate set of poem-letters, each a dense block of text full of the vocative 'O', archaisms, affectations, repetitions and fragments of Greek and Latin. The poems are thick with references to philosophy, art, history and much more. This can all seem intimidating, but because they are written as letters the tone is warm and convivial. Lehóczky gives us complicated references for titles, providing a shadowy context that abstracts more than it explains. Are we meant to seek out an underlying narrative of writer, recipient and cataloguer, or bask in the drama of the language on the page, in writing about swimming as writing about swimming?

> [...] let's
> continue to be patient, since today's swim is another
> attempt to do it well on the page. To navigate the body
> home through language. To home in on the world.
> ('[+ Prologos: [Apostil 1 / Illuminations 1]')

Everywhere we turn there is a swimmer – at once self and other, the problematic lyric I, the forebear who the writer must write against, and the ideal poet and poem behind the reality:

> [...] the
> original, the archetypal swimmer inside the
> swimmer inside we long to find.
> ('[PE x; letter X:13]')

This "silent swimmer" is described negatively: "*sans* silhouette, *sans* soul" ('PE ii; letter II:13'). This recalls Jacques's speech in *As You Like It* and highlights a preoccupation with the body, mortality and decay: "The split second before the body / turns" ('[PE vi; letter VI:13]'). This is actually a paraphrase of a quote from the artist Helen Chadwick, whose work Lehóczky references and meditates on in these poems, drawing parallels with other artworks including Hieronymus Bosch's *The Garden of Earthly Delights*. The pool is also described as "*sans*", existing between the real pools of Budapest, the ideal pool and the metaphorical pool, it is "Pool emptiful" ('[PE iii; letter III:13]'), suspended, like everything in these poems, between presence and absence.

There is a great deal going on in this sequence, large volumes of matter compressed and fermenting, as in Chadwick's 'Carcass'. At times I wished the heady currents of ideas would resolve into an essay, but *Pool Epitaphs* seems to be an exercise in resistance, framing, distancing at every level. When I interrogate the possible reasons for this sequence being written and presented the way it is I find I cannot defend my disinclination for the work: it is theoretically sound. And yet I am still bothered by an earnestness not quite earned, a playfulness that feels pushy. Perhaps this comes from the sense that there was no room for me in these poems – they already seem to have a reader there, one who knows everything they need to know without going off to google artists and Greek phrases in order to break through the meniscus. The reader is secondary because the text is already ghosted with readers, recipients, editors, cataloguers. And so I drifted between admiration and annoyance. I struggled. I splashed. I dived in from different angles, paddled, puzzled, took a breath and submerged myself again. I found myself sometimes enjoying and sometimes hating the experience, found myself giving up and then coming back, finding that "the pool is closed / and open too like a script with open ending" ('[PE ix; letter IX:13]').

My copy of Elizabeth-Jane Burnett's *Swims* has been carried around in my rucksack so that it has become damp, dirty and somewhat tattered. This feels appropriate because I think of the collection as a handbook, full as it is with guidelines or suggestions for being in and thinking about our environment. The first poem – or section, again this is not a book that splits easily into poem 'parts' – is a list of definitions of "To Swim". These immediately signal the range of references and concerns that Burnett employs, blending sensation and thought, the personal and the political, the man-made and the natural:

To drift.
To not advance   capitalism.
To grow in a hedge.
To be lichen.
To be at once
in the body
and under
and over it.

The form disintegrates as we turn the page. This untitled poem precedes the 'Preface', an instance of the delay and framing that continues throughout the collection. One long sequence gives the book its form, a poem broken into parts and following twelve wild swims across England and Wales. The idea of interruption is important with the phrase *"Swimming is continuous, only the rivers are intermittent"* occurring right at the end as well as near the start of the collection, presented like a quote but enigmatically unidentified.

Burnett revels in a great diversity of approaches. Compare 'The English Channel', where the non-human is explored by riffing on the words of Arthur Ransome, with the lyrical couplets of 'The Barle':

[...] in Fukushima, where fishermen

record radioactive caesium in fish,
three years after the earthquake,

three years on from the tsunami:
I can no more take this out

of the poem as out of the water.

Burnett presents her processes as if mimicking the scientific research she often makes use of in her work. In 'The Teign' she quotes from a local fisheries survey and then gives a set of five points to show her methods for writing the poem. The outcome is an amended version of the same survey, Burnett's thoughts intruding into the text like non-native species in a waterway:

Molluscs and Crustaceans are very rare indeed, although isolated pockets of **guilt** do occur [...]

Other "problems" pollute the report: the Arctic, migraines, fear of sinking. Burnett manages to be overtly political without being simplistic. And the act of swimming is itself political, for to be in lakes and rivers is to transgress, "to explode column width of day's database, expand with joy in the / margins... // Is to be where people had not planned you to be" ('Grasmere').

Cradled in the centre of the collection are the three 'Poems for My Father', prompted, we are told, by the illness of Burnett's father and situated in the Aegean Sea – which has its own mythical currents. These are distinctly different, shorter, more oblique in some ways but also more direct:

> [...] A battering of pear
> scents air as I scull a memory where
> you used to sell wallflowers [...]
> ('Wallflowers')

After this short interlude we return to the UK, but this personal pain – and the rhyming used in describing it – flows out into the other poems. In the final poem, 'The Dart', a recurrence of grief for the father is refigured as gratitude:

> there is a glimpse of an orange armband and an arm missing
> from a waist that turned to see him watch as I pulled away
> for the first time unaided into wildness [...]

This book refreshes like an icy dip, startling us from both comfort and despair. Burnett's poems invite the reader into the water with them; to take action, accept responsibility, and find joy: "it is all yours, this open possibility."

Emily Hasler swims mostly in the Essex Stour. Her first collection, The Built Environment, *will be published by Pavilion in 2018.*

FLUNG OUT SOLO

Amaan Hyder, At Hajj, *Penned in the Margins, £9.99,*
ISBN *9781908058447*
Rachel McCrum, The First Blast to Awaken Women Degenerate,
Freight, *£9.99,* ISBN *9781911332428*
Claudine Toutoungi, Smoothie, Carcanet, *£9.99,*
ISBN *9781784104122*

Mary Jean Chan finds dexterity, complexity and deft imagery in
three debuts

. . .

These three debut collections are all deeply concerned with the human body and its responses to experiences ranging from the religious to the mundane. Amaan Hyder's *At Hajj* juxtaposes the repetitive and incantatory nature of the annual pilgrimage to Mecca (one of the five pillars of Islam) with brief lyrical interludes which meditate on the complexities of language, family and cultural inheritance. The central sequence of the collection is made up of simple yet elegant prose-poems which depict daily scenes from the Hajj – austere and spartan episodes conveyed from a third-person perspective – which are suspended momentarily in language as mise-en-scènes of "people standing to pray, putting their hands on their knees and drawing up and going down to touch their foreheads to the ground".

In a blog piece written for Penned in the Margins, Hyder reveals that his connection to the Hajj is a vicarious rather than personal one, for he began to write about the annual pilgrimage after reflecting deeply upon reading a newspaper article about the Hajj, watching a television programme which tracked a group of pilgrims, and speaking to relatives and friends who had either already returned or were making plans to go. As such, the reader encounters these retellings as if listening intently to a traveller's tale, somewhat akin to the sensations evoked by Italo Calvino's *Invisible Cities* (1972), a book of prose poems which powerfully blends fact and fiction through the recollections of the explorer Marco Polo. In a similar fashion, Hyder expertly conjures up the Hajj in a deeply immersive experience wherein one's emotional, physical and spiritual relationship to another human being is rendered in a series of dreamlike recollections strung between reality and myth:

> *He had been in his own group walking in a line with his hands around the waist of the man in front. His group had been snaking through the crowds like that for a few days. One morning he had been at the back of the line and he had felt the crowds closing in. He had not seen it bottleneck so badly before. The message went down the line to hold on tight and he had the sweat of the man in front on his beard.*
>
> *[...]*
>
> *I've seen him asking around for his people, that man. The orphan. He had been in his own group, walking in a line with his hands around the waist of the man in front. He says in his language that he is lost. And watches while the message he sends out goes down the line like a boy scrambling on shoulders in a crowd. The scent bottlenecks at his beard and in his sleep he is lost and lifted and let go in the cried-out desert.*

The First Blast to Awaken Women Degenerate by Rachel McCrum offers a more fluid range of thematic concerns, many of which concern the (cis-) female body's relationship to a world saturated with sexual violence. In the collection's title poem, the speaker responds directly to a misogynistic epigraph by John Knox: "The First Blast of the Trumpet Against the Monstrous Regiment of Women" (1558), but also takes as its impetus more recent events "of mass sexual violence against women" around the globe which inspired McCrum's "absolute terror of groups of men" (as she comments on the Dangerous Women Project blog). The poem begins uneasily, but soon finds its decided rhythm and heartbeat towards the middle in a litany of war-cries:

> Give me gorilla women and bear women
> penguin women and wolf hound women
>
> blue whale women and badger women
> yeti, yak and bison women
>
> Give me caribou women and bone women
> bite back beefy women
> ('The First Blast to Awaken Women Degenerate')

In this collection, it is the poems on familial relationships that sing best, including meditations on McCrum's Irish and Scottish roots. However, not all her poems manage to avoid the pitfalls associated with straightforward diction. In 'The last rhino', lines such as "The bewilderment in the hang / of that bouldering head / would break your heart and mine" come across as emotionally unconvincing despite the poem's weighty subject matter. Lyricism is not a certain feature throughout the book, but McCrum is certainly capable of deft imagery:

> Meanwhile, my brother searches for celestial runways.
> When duelling galaxies clash with enough violence,
> some bodies, willing or not, are flung out solo.
>
> [...]
>
> Look harder. There is more in the sky
> than you see at first glance.
> Between the galaxies, light seeps.
> ('Runways')

Likewise, in the final poem, the speaker mingles pathos with keen observation:

> The first time I flew to you,
> the plane passed over a graveyard

before hitting the runway.
I flew towards that dawn in a tin tube
full of strangers and thin air.

('Time difference')

Claudine Toutoungi's *Smoothie* features speakers knee-deep in the idiosyncrasies of language and linguistic play as they explore their common ailments of loneliness, desire and heartbreak. The opening poem offers a darkly comic take on one's desperate need to be loved or simply seen, as the speaker resolutely declares:

Because I think you'd like me better as an artefact
I sit for ages in the sculpture park.
Flies settle on my arms.

[...]

This is for real. I shall remain here,
unmoved by sheep and hedge trimmers,
until you notice me.

('This is Not a Fad')

The lack of gender binaries or sexist undertones in this poem enables the reader to empathise to an extent with the speaker's act of self-objectification. The juxtaposition of "sculpture park" and "flies" in the opening stanza effectively conjures up the image of an individual immobilised in their unrequited yearning, somewhat akin to Viola/Cesario in Shakespeare's *Twelfth Night* who "never told her love, / But let concealment, like a worm i' the bud, / Feed on her damask cheek. She pined in thought, / And with a green and yellow melancholy / She sat like patience on a monument, / Smiling at grief" (II.iv.108–113). Here, the flies appear to be modernised (and more likely) versions of Shakespeare's worms, both equally repugnant as symbols of the external world's indifference towards human desire.

Given Toutoungi's dexterity with clipped lines and terse observations, it is refreshing to encounter a few poems in this collection which offer more opportunities for skilful enjambment and flowing sentences. In 'Skirting', the speaker observes a surrealist scene of domestic discord, depicted with a keen intensity which stretches time and heightens the reader's sense of colour, atmosphere and texture:

Somewhere,
potentially a roof terrace or gazebo,
preferably a contained space with a certain quantity of sunlight
bleaching the architecture,
two people are skirting the issue.

[...]

Ideally, a butterfly grazing an ear
permits an intake of breath
or tense hiatus,

but if climate change or an increase in
urbanization has put an end to fluttering,
if nothing is left in the air, save a trace of jasmine,

the skirting will still grow more urgent,
dextrous. It will ricochet.
It will become the butterfly.

I admire the tightly controlled pacing of this poem, how it slows down then gathers speed to mimic the ways in which an argument might unfold between two people. The butterfly functions as a curious symbol in the poem's last few lines – beginning as a gentle reminder that a larger world exists beyond "the skirting" taking place, then disappearing suddenly as a result of the speaker's thought experiment on climate catastrophe and species extinction. The turn at the end of the poem is welcome because of its metaphorical ingenuity – how "the skirting" might become so frenzied that it "become[s] the butterfly". Such metaphors are deeply satisfying because they are skilfully rendered, in Mark Waldron's words, with "a lightness of touch". Towards the end of the collection, the speaker offers a gorgeous description of an unrequited lover: "You're there in front of me / looking like the longest, tallest / coolest glass of water" ('Reunion'). Reading Toutoungi's collection feels, in more ways than one, like indulging in a long, cool drink, only to be occasionally surprised by its intriguing yet refreshing aftertaste.

Mary Jean Chan is a co-editor of Oxford Poetry *and was recently selected as a Ledbury Emerging Critic.*

SEE YOURSELF

Shane McCrae, In the Language of My Captor, *Wesleyan, $24.95,*
ISBN 9780819577115
Ishaq Imruh Bakari, Without Passport or Apology, *Smokestack,*
£7.99, ISBN 9780995563544

Edward Doegar on two collections exploring the legacy of slavery
and colonialism

. . .

"When have you not had to say / Something about white
folks to say / Something about me" ('BANJO YES ASKS A
JOURNALIST'). This question, from Shane McCrae's *In the
Language of My Captor*, seems to anticipate the book's reception. In one
way or another, it's the subject of every poem in the book. Take 'BANJO YES
RECEIVES A LIFETIME ACHIEVEMENT AWARD', in which the title character of the
sequence acquires his name. On a film lot (a pre-Civil Rights Act
Hollywood studio, I presume, though pointedly the dates are withheld)
the character hears

                         a shout
     Banjo and so   I lift my head but not

     Too high that ain't my name and I say *Yes*
     Back loud but   real polite

Seeing that the white boy who called "Banjo" is lifting one leg slightly "like he was / Limping standing still", the speaker runs over:

> I run quick o-
> ver to him I say *Yes sir* tells me to
> Bend down and wipe this   is the truth it was
>
> A spot of bird shit from his shoe
> this ain't   / No kind of story where the nigger says
> *No* I bent down and cleaned his shoe

Finally, the humiliation is ritualised into baptism:

> Smiling he says *Is your name Banjo* I
> Say *No sir my name's Bill* and he   says *Ban-*
>
> *jo suits you better   Banjo Yes   and when*
> *I talk to you that's who you're gonna be*

Though he never sees his tormentor again, this new name sticks – expanding that white boy's 'I' into the world's view of Bill/Banjo. McCrae is masterful at allowing the particular to bleed into the general like this, for anecdote to acquire the force of allegory. Finally, Bill/Banjo explains he has never had to "act" the subservient roles that he was subsequently offered, noting: "A white boy talking on the screen   that's him / And when you see me smiling back that's me". Later, the character concludes that "You can be free / Or you can live", which sounds like hyperbole, but isn't. Instead, it recalls the first sequence in the book: a set of fables on slavery, all the more prescient for their ahistorical setting. In these poems the captive, a black man, is relating his experience in a white man's zoo. In 'PANOPTICON', he reflects that "The keeper put me in the cage   with the monkeys". But despite this state of surveillance, the captive recognises what the supposedly free cannot see: "*Whether you're here / to see me   or to see the monkeys // You're here to see yourself*". For McCrae, the hegemony of white American culture makes victims of both the captives and captors; though unequal victims, of course. The paradoxes of this captivity are explored; the reliance on the system in order to challenge the system, such as the captive explaining what he refuses to say:

I *cannot* talk about the place I came from
I do not want it to exist
The way I knew it
In the language of my captor

('IN THE LANGUAGE')

Every poem in the book seems to risk something, seems to have come at a cost. This is particularly true of the major central sequence, which intersperses prose memoir from McCrae's distressing childhood with historical personae poems. The historical poems are voiced by Jefferson Davis (the president of the Confederacy), and Jim Limber (his adoptive mixed-race son). Davis's wife, Varina, on seeing a mixed-race child being beaten by his black mother, "rescued" the child, taking the boy home and renaming him Jim Limber. This strangely echoes the actions of McCrae's own ("white supremacist") maternal grandfather who took the young McCrae from his (black) father's home. Both boys were beaten and abused in different ways: "Momma Varina rescued me   she whups me / Different   like what she wants from it is love" ('JIM LIMBER THE ADOPTED MULATTO SON OF JEFFERSON DAVIS MET HIS ADOPTIVE MOTHER VARINA DAVIS AT A CROSSROADS');

> When I was a child, I was willing, even eager, to let anybody do anything they wanted to me, so long as they didn't hurt me, and so long as what they were doing looked like the things I saw people doing in my grandfather's magazines
>
> ('PURGATORY: A MEMOIR / A SON AND A FATHER OF SONS', PART 2)

The interwoven elements exchange properties. The Civil War-era monologues take on the living urgency of contemporary abuse, while McCrae's own testimony becomes more of a historical document, oddly estranged from its first-person narration. The abuse he describes becomes, in part, a consequence of historical precedent.

Such sensitive subject matter is exquisitely handled by McCrae. He seems wary of creating any new opportunities for the white supremacist tactic of reading a black subject as an object. In 'BANJO YES RECEIVES A LIFETIME ACHIEVEMENT AWARD', the reader is forced to concentrate on the act of reading; the use of the virgule as a marker of the metrical count (often printed mid-line) insists on a dialogue between intention and tradition.

Likewise the awkward punctuation and spacing remind us that what we are doing is literally *making sense* of the act described; the little shocks of narrative are redoubled by the miscues. The aim isn't to reinscribe the hate depicted but to make it more felt; it is excruciatingly successful. This is a riveting and necessary book.

Ishaq Imruh Bakari's third book of poems, *Without Passport or Apology*, also explores the present moment as the living legacy of slavery, empire and colonialism. It has a huge scope of reference, taking in historical and contemporary poems set in Rwanda, Zanzibar, Haiti, Liberia, Paris, Tanzania and throughout the Caribbean. Again, like McCrae, Bakari is interested in examining how white supremacist attitudes continue to dictate people's lives today:

> indecent as the glare
> of a lynch mob
> Africa hangs suited
> and tied swaying in submission
> without peace
> dumbfounded by the juju of maps
>   ('The Border')

These poems are overtly political, tracing the ways in which the historical crimes of empire have created the ground for contemporary capitalism, exploited now by corrupt governments and cronyism: so roads are built only "for fast moving motorcades / and presidents rushing away / from the governed mass" past "investors licensed to rob" ('The Marketplace'). At their best the poems bluntly call out the practical reality of inequality:

> his life like local music
> is officially worth
> no more than a one night
> hotel room in low season
>   ('After the Rain')

Reducing life to insurable value is particularly unpleasant when quantified in terms of exchange rates.

Another poem speaks in the voice of Dedan Kimathi (who led the Mau Mau uprising in Kenya against the British in the 1950s): "in the silhouette

I am the black / missing from the union jack". This sort of neat agitprop slogan plays to Bakari's strengths and it's convincing. But the bluntness has too little variety to be consistently effective: it becomes dull. There's a sense of 'Yes, *and?*' Bakari's poetic technique simply isn't subtle enough to do credit to his genuinely impressive historical and cultural understanding. Consider the poems' complete lack of punctuation: initially it's a relief that it reads so easily, but soon the fluidity becomes soporific – there is rarely any pressure in the lines, no need to retrace the path of a thought. Equally, his metaphors have the short arm's reach of cliché: "time / was already ticking / blood / was already boiling". The lineation underlines already emphatic phrasing: "in the dawn / there is sunset / in the infinite void / volcanoes weep". Short quasi-nursery-rhyme lines ("There was once / a young boy / who often stood" etc.) give way to the prosaic clarification ("school books seeking a route / to a more desirable disembarkation") for no discernible reason. At worst, the poems read like bad translations from juvenilia: "Inside the solitude of your silence [...] a fresh breeze / Warmed by a melodic note of your music // A rare moment of truth".

It's a pity. Bakari has important things to say but hasn't found a way to say them. Even atrocities need to be interesting. The linguistic pressure just isn't enough – often the language could be paraphrased in prose without a substantial loss of effect. The result is angry, well-meant, but diffuse. In contrast, Shane McCrae's book is exquisitely held together, its feelings and thought bound by lyric precision: it is one of the best books I've read this year.

Edward Doegar's pamphlet, For Now, *is published by clinic.*

THE WORDS ON EVERY SIGN ARE STRANGE

Jenny Danes, Gaps, smith/doorstop, £5, ISBN 9781910367971
Edward Doegar, For Now, clinic, £5.99, ISBN 9780993318252
Padraig Regan, Who Seemed Alive & Altogether Real,
Emma Press, £6.50, ISBN 9781910139745
Rhian Edwards, Brood, Seren, £6, ISBN 9781781724217
Theophilus Kwek, The First Five Storms, smith/doorstop, £5,
ISBN 9781910367728

Jennifer Wong considers music, experiment, myth-making and
more in five new pamphlets

. . .

Jenny Danes's *Gaps* haunts with its music and honesty. Danes creates an uncanny language for gaps: from a sense of estrangement in a foreign city or tongue, to the loneliness of the body. In 'This is what it feels like', the poet imagines becoming a wall that is "untouchable, unpatterned / and hard to breathe through", and observes that "[p]eople are very ignorant / I'm not really exempting myself from that". In 'November', the narrator contrasts the composed expressions of others with a sense of being "scraped out on the inside". Recalling a teacher's remark – "*I like the way Jennifer tried to spell 'anxious'*" – the poem questions our faith in language and love:

If the words on every sign are strange, should you just shut your eyes?
What about failing to eavesdrop and putting on headphones? What
    about love?
If we can't survive being buried in each other's mother tongue
maybe we should abandon the rest, close our hearts and mouths

Danes's poems are imbued with texture and immediacy. In 'Deutsch',
the poet muses on the strangeness of German terms translated into
English: "What goes down? A glow pear, an ice bear, away sickness, / a
rain shield, a strike wood to make a flame." Balancing philosophical
questions and self-doubt with the hope of healing, Danes demonstrates
how poetic language can inhabit different spaces and meanings.

Edward Doegar's *For Now* is a bold experiment with satirical language.
In 'Answers', he mocks our inability to escape class prejudices: "What we
can't help but notice / That the poor grow senile / Differently". His
disciplined economy of language questions stereotypes and looks for ways
to reconcile differences. In taut tercets, 'Portrayal: A Double Portrait' satirises
those blinded by their superiority: "Asia is a single thought / It is iceberg-
blue." In 'Lonely Planet', he makes ironic statements about cities based on
found text from tourist guidebooks: "Sarajevo is intriguing / And
cosmopolitan". By imitating tourist-speak, the poet alludes to the
impossibility of understanding another culture without actually immersing
oneself in it. In 'The Sanctioned State', he evokes the terrorist demolition
of Baal's Temple in Syria, mocking 'our' self-righteousness and ignorance:
"Jesus is not Muhammad". The poem concludes: "But there is no we / No
consensus / Just my own / Finger pointing / At an imagined face". The
contrasting pronouns articulate the problem of a democratic society: the
lack of consensus goes hand in hand with the individual's right to choose.
The pamphlet ends with 'A Demonstration', in which Doegar rounds up
his linguistic adventure – "Safe / Is the last / Adjective" – a line that echoes
his willingness to take measured risks with form in this intelligent debut.

Marked by the use of collaged imagery, Padraig Regan's *Who Seemed
Alive & Altogether Real* destabilises meanings through myth-making. As
Andrew McMillan points out in the introduction, one moves through
Regan's poems "in the same way one should around a gallery", adjusting
one's gaze from time to time. The title-poem sequence questions the divide
between the real and the imagined. In 'Boy with a Basket of Fruit', the
poet dwells on Caravaggio's choice to have "[a] boy instead of table"

holding the basket of fruits, and wonders about the conventions of the time ("I forget the convention / was not yet established: / no one even thought of tables then"). In 'Hibiscus', Regan conjures an intimate portrait of Jean Cocteau, a French poet and artist fascinated with Classical myths. In the poem, Cocteau resurrects a ripped-up hibiscus ("He inserts the stamen") and inspires Regan across time and space ("Later he'll say / that he liked my first poem / about Jean Cocteau; / this was a lie"). In his 'Johann Zoffany' sequence the poet creates new dialogue between artists. In 'Johann Zoffany Goes for a Swim with David Hockney', Regan practically inserts the German Neoclassical painter Zoffany into Hockney's iconic swimming pool painting ("The huge heat of the California sun already drying his shoulders"). Spread horizontally across the page, the poem compels us to adjust our gaze. The bemused voice shifts effortlessly between the past and the present against a canvas of magical realism. In such original ways, Regan makes poetry a deliberate, performative act.

In *Brood*, Rhian Edwards explores the labour of love through imaginative accounts of birds' lives, recalling medieval conventions of bird imagery. The pamphlet begins with 'The Birds of Rhiannon', which revolves around Celtic myths of magical birds that belong to the goddess Rhiannon, who "serenades / the dead from their dreams, lullabying / the living to torpor". In the myth-retelling, Edwards details the birds' human-like affections and sufferings: "For the sake of my world and him, / I crowded my belly with children." The ten-part sequence 'Pied Margot' transforms with originality some of the best-known rhymes for magpies. In 'Silver', she articulates the sorrow of the unloved mistress – "Never one to grasp the whimsy of dearness" – whose longing for love leads her to the compromised resignation to accept a "secondhand proposal / with the regalia of a Coke ring". In 'Joy', she brings to life the delight of intimacy:

The foiling of your solitude's ruin,
is enough to make me press
this quivering, dealt hand
to the birdcage barring my heart.

Navigating the joys and sorrows in love – from courtship and promises to separations – Edwards highlights the body as a vessel of emotions and fertility. The sequence 'A Bird That's Best to Miss' shifts the perspective to that of the expectant mother, who observes the strangeness of her pregnant body in early morning and her loneliness to feel the "blank half" of the bed, a time "too dark for bird / song".

A debut by Singaporean-born poet Theophilus Kwek, *The First Five Storms* evokes a melancholic yet beautiful landscape steeped in history and nostalgia. Kwek has an excellent ear for music, and he channels this music into a spare, nuanced language. 'Requiem', a eulogy to a late grandfather, conveys the missing of the dead, and the living quality of memory: "Teach me now to love, at their frayed ends / the left-behind, their washed and ashen fingers." In 'Sophia', the poet revisits the colonial history of Singapore from Sir Thomas Raffles's letter to his wife, a reimagined account of "the pearl of our possessions" from the coloniser's perspective. In the main sequence in the pamphlet, 'The First Five Storms', the poet interweaves the passage of a storm with the speaker's emotional landscape:

> [...] and such a calm
> of winter, road-pressed tracks, a dark *bonsai*
> stopped by a window of our chimneyed home.
> We stood, then went in our cars to church,
> and scraped our shoes, and left the dog outside.

The delicate tension between the internal and the external, between one's immediate experience of the world and an eclipsed future, is sustained by the subtle, seamless shifts in perspective and imagery. This sense of continuity and shared wisdom between the human and the natural world is also reflected in 'The Weaver', where "creatures love and, like us, try / to bind the ones they love", or in 'What Follows' in which a deer that turns to escape from the predator is "on the flint of that eternity / more alive than in the burnished wood". Through measured and elusive verse, Kwek articulates the proximity of history in tender, personal terms.

Jennifer Wong is currently completing a PhD on place and identity in contemporary Chinese diaspora poetry at Oxford Brookes University.

CANS AND DESERT THISTLES

Terence Tiller, The Collected Poems, *Eyewear, £20,*
ISBN 9781911335405

Rory Waterman looks back over the work of a neglected modernist

. . .

Terence Tiller (1916–1987) was once a poet of some repute, largely as a result of his poems from Egypt during the Second World War; he has since fallen into obscurity – rarely anthologised, and routinely ignored in discussions of war poetry. He published six collections: three between 1941 and 1947, while he worked as a lecturer in Cairo, and the others back in his native England, where he worked for the BBC. The stated aim of this handsome book is to bring back into print, in his centenary year, the complete body of work of what the book's (and press's) editor, Todd Swift, proclaims to be "a rediscovered lyric-modernist genius".

Swift's introduction is informative about the first three books, but doesn't extend to a discussion of the others – or, to put it another way, to the last three decades of the four represented in the volume. The result is that the introduction feels half-done, for all that it is long and laudatory, variously marking Tiller out as a "quintessential poet of the Forties style" (with some justification), the originator of the Movement style long before "its ostensible origins in 1950s Britain", and a modernist too modern to be appreciated by his contemporaries. His response to the sometimes lukewarm reception Tiller received in the 1940s is to "wonder if what we have here is a failure of criticism itself at the period – a moment [A.T.] Tolley, [Alan] Ross and others could not conceive of a different style, another modern way". Tiller, Swift argues, was simply too brilliantly original to be understood properly at the time – as J.C. Squire with Eliot's *The Waste Land*, so Tolley and Ross with Tiller, whose work "simply blows all critical fuses". It's a shame Swift can't celebrate Tiller for the significant but wholeheartedly minor poet he was. His comments hardly prepare us for 'For Doreen', the opener to *Poems* (1941):

> *Time is the medium, not the kind,*
> *of dreaming in the actual tense;*
> *under the dreams you will not find*
> *their being, but their imminence.*

Such formal decorousness, and conventional sentiment, are not at odds with many other poems here, despite the lonely, Eliotian *flâneurie* and abrupt shifts in tone that also typify this and other of Tiller's collections. The earliest work is frequently undermined by wailing, epiphanic romanticism and over-poeticised youthful angst of a fairly silly kind – "look down stars, you illimitable and glorious wakers, / on her delight that wakes from silks", or "Now as I lie, owls in the dark gardens / – swift for destroying, sudden circlers – wail / for no grief; trees have their windy burdens"; and on it goes. Occasionally, this contemplative spirit is turned with grim determination to overbearing worldly concerns, though often vaguely or abstractly:

> The world is weary of harness now,
> the open, the tumultuous:
> shutter the window, let the bough
> be plucked that blossoms God knows how.
> The smell of death is over us.

Another intriguing early poem is the overlong 'Egypt 1940', with its cleverly altering refrains – "The night finds us the body betrays us / and love devours us and time passes", "The body betrays us and love devours us / and time passes and none saves us" – and its sense of being at a unique remove from "the sharp / and screaming rack of Europe".

Prefacing *The Inward Animal* (1943), Tiller wrote that the war's "impact and the impact of strangeness must have shaken, and destroyed, many a customary self". The collection has a tripartite structure at once obvious and *sui generis*: "distress; rebellion against place and circumstance; slow mutual absorption ending in the birth of something at once myself and a new self and Egypt". He is a war poet writing from a position unlike others – involved and yet not, and on a particular margin. Many of the poems here are linked to specific North African locations, such as 'Coptic Church' (set in 'Musturrud'), which evokes the "memory of magnificence" that "reared up this primitive pretence". The collection is more formally adventurous than his first, but drops regularly into the same pitfalls of prolixity and abstraction, as in the title poem:

> The primitive revolt
> against a mind or will,
> the blood of Abel spilt
> in cups already full.
> Being and feeling and thought
> are but a naked man
> who fights what he is not,
> the animal within.

Simultaneously, the younger Tiller is prone to philosophising maxims, often boldly wearing the urgent influence of MacSpaunday: 'World was not built for dreams' recalls McNeice's 'Snow', and the line "World is suddener than we fancy it"; elsewhere, he warns "Never believe us, poets tell you lies". He certainly takes on the big questions and has something to say about them, but it doesn't always sound like him speaking.

In these first two books, most poems are numbered; for *Unarm, Eros* (1947), Tiller abandons numbering, so each poem seems more a discrete entity, and adopts a more quizzical tone and often a narrower focus. Many of the poems are still fuelled by the least answerable questions and attendant simmering anxieties. Elsewhere, attention is given to unease at the poet's relationship to the war in comparison to most other temporary British expatriates in North Africa. In the acutely observed and moving 'Lecturing to Troops', "strange violent men" whom the speaker has come to address "sit like shrubs among the cans and desert thistles", with "dirty unfamiliar muscles", "wanting girls and beer". Before them, he is "shy" and guilt-ridden: "They have walked horror's coast", while "I come taut and scatheless with a virgin air". The sweeping generalisations about these men reveal his own vulnerability and alienation. Other moments of observation are less successful, such as the obvious irony in 'Beggar' of a hand held "out like an offering"; but this collection marks the high point of Tiller's poetry: he has plenty to say, and has by this point developed a talent for understated formal control that usually keeps his probing meditations in check.

A decade passed before *Reading a Medal, and Other Poems* (1957), by which time Tiller had long since returned home. The poems are again often inquisitively anxious to see the details of things but also to posit ecumenical questions – as in 'Tropical Aquarium', which begins with "the absurd / flexes of small and coloured flesh" and ends "Must I be glad, having seen them lose the wings / that swam with rainbows, rainbows floating: them?" To Tiller, such questions are also questions of faith, as explored in poems such as 'Three Christmas Trees', which moves from the candle-lit "tree of night" to a sleeping son: "There is no age in sleep; the boy is one / with infant and with patriarch". The poem then imagines the child "companion to that other boy / whose parents' dreams lay round him as he slept". It is as beautiful as it is conventional.

Of course, this collection lacks the Egyptian wartime contexts that render some of the earlier poems more than the sum of their parts, but it is otherwise another high point, when Tiller was most completely in control of form and subject. At times, it owes much to Philip Larkin and the typically understated Movement aesthetic – and there is even a controlled, moving poem about Victorian street performers that, like Larkin's 'Deceptions', published two years earlier, grows from a passage in Henry Mayhew's *London Labour and the London Poor*, 1851.

How often do older poets appear to run out of things to say, or new ways to say things, their work seeming suddenly slipshod? Tiller is not among the countless exceptions, and his final two collections, *Notes for a Myth* (1968) and *That Singing Mesh* (1979), are on the whole weaker and less interesting. In the former, Tiller is again at his best when moving from a focus on minutiae to the existential questions served up by his intense and religious mindset, as in 'Keepsakes', in which the "golden locket-glass" of amber, with its "fossil grief", becomes a counterpart to our transience. In a foreword, Tiller explains that *That Singing Mesh* is to be his final volume, and makes "an earnest plea to friends who may possess poems of mine [...] other than these printed here: destroy them". (None appear in the *Collected*.) It abounds with sonnets and villanelles – one of Tiller's favoured forms – and, unusually, notes to poems, though not always the most helpful sort: "In these villanelles it will be found that each repetition of the refrains has a slightly different meaning", one begins, as though this is not usual for villanelles with any merit, the repetends acting as hinges rather than largely redundant placeholders. Unfortunately, Tiller's often fall short of his wish for them:

> The most of pain is greater than its need;
> but who shall draw the colours from the glass
> until the firing becomes death indeed?
>
> To snatch reluctant wings is baby greed
> (lust is foundry that unfuses brass):
> the most of pain is greater than its need.

It is odd for a poet to know he is writing the last poems he'll preserve, but, for all its obliquity, the closing title poem offers little doubt about his intentions: "the last music in the sky shall be / a breaking string; and then the axes' fall". Yes: multiple axes. And with that, Tiller ended an intriguing if deeply flawed body of work, amounting to about 270 pages.

These are not the final poems in the book, however, which closes with appendices containing poems by the poet's daughter Sarah Tiller and his grandson Matthew, in addition to seventeen monochrome photographs of the poet, taken at various points in his life, including one of him in old age smiling beside a child who might be Matthew (though the caption doesn't tell us, and is apparently misdated "1954"). Matthew Tiller's prefatory note stresses that the extra poems are included "at Todd [Swift]'s suggestion", and that he hopes the book will be judged solely by his grandfather's work. They are nice enough and well meant; but so do I.

It is far-fetched to pretend Terence Tiller is a major poet, or even an especially good one. For all that, he is interesting, primarily because of the time and place of his early adulthood and the sensibility he brought to bear on it in his poems. He deserves to be read and studied in that context.

Rory Waterman's second collection is Sarajevo Roses *(Carcanet, 2017).*

CODA

Remembering the many magnificent poets who have left us this year
with this selection of portraits. © Chris Riddell

DEREK
WALCOTT

TOM
RAWORTH

SARAH
MAGUIRE

HELEN
DUNMORE

JOHN
ASHBERY

ROY
FISHER

JAMES
BERRY

CONTRIBUTORS

Paul Birtill has published a number of collections with Hearing Eye • **Dzifa Benson** was born in London to Ghanaian parents and grew up in several countries in West Africa. She is a poet, writer, theatre-maker, producer and journalist • **Louis Bourne** is Professor Emeritus of Spanish at Georgia College and State University; his translation of Andrés Sánchez Robayna's *The Book, Behind the Dune* (Shearsman, 2017) was a PBS Recommendation • **Hisham Bustani** is an award-winning poet and short-story writer from Jordan • **Kayo Chingonyi** is Poetry Editor at *The White Review*. His first full-length collection, *Kumukanda*, was published by Chatto & Windus in 2017 • **Julia Copus** is working on a new collection and a biography of turn-of-the-century poet Charlotte Mew • **Lucia Dove** is half-Russian, and currently lives in Amsterdam where she works for Amsterdam University Press • **Thoraya El-Rayyes** is a Palestinian-Canadian literary translator who specialises in bringing Arabic literature from the Levant into English • **Carrie Etter**'s fourth collection, *The Weather in Normal*, will be published by Seren in 2018 • **O. Flote** was born in southern Africa, as were his parents and grandparents. He currently lives in Tasmania • **Linda France**'s latest collection is *Reading the Flowers* (Arc, 2016) • **Richard Georges** is the author of *Make Us All Islands* (Shearsman, 2017) and *Giant* (Platypus, forthcoming). He lives and works in the British Virgin Islands • **Joanna Guthrie** writes poetry and non-fiction. Her first collection is *Billack's Bones* (The Rialto, 2007). Her second, *Water Person Kit*, is forthcoming • **Jen Hadfield** teaches Creative Writing at the University of Glasgow and is building a house in Shetland • **Will Harris**'s debut pamphlet is *All this is implied* (HappenStance, 2017), and his work can be found in the anthology *Ten: Poets of the New Generation* (Bloodaxe, 2017) • **Ian Humphreys** won the Hamish Canham Prize 2016 and is a fellow of The Complete Works III • **Jang Su-Jin** was included in Moonji's 12th *Literature and Intelligence Selected Poets* series, and her book of poems is scheduled for release in 2017 from Moonji • **Jae Kim** lives in St Louis and teaches fiction writing as a Third-Year Fellow at Washington University, where he recently finished his MFA • **Melissa Lee-Houghton** lives in Blackburn, Lancashire. Her latest collection, *Sunshine* (Penned in the Margins, 2016), won the Somerset Maugham Award • **Lee Young-Ju**'s books of poetry include *108th Man* (Munhakdongne, 2005), *My Dear Older Sister* (Minumsa, 2010), and *Cold Candies* (Moonji, 2014) • **Dave Margoshes** is a Canadian poet and fiction-writer living on a Saskatchewan farm • **Juan Nicolás Padrón** was born in Cuba in 1951. His many collections include *Crónica de la noche* (News from the Night, 1995) and *La llegada de los dioses* (The Arrival of the Gods,2008) • **Holly Pester** is a poet living mostly in London. She is working on her first full collection on bogs and abortivity and is Lecturer in Poetry and Performance at University of Essex • **Kate Potts**'s second poetry collection, *Feral*, will be published by Bloodaxe in 2018 • **Billy Ramsell**'s second collection, *The Architect's Dream of Winter* (Dedalus, 2013), was shortlisted for the 2014 Irish

Times/Poetry Now award. He lives in Cork • **Penelope Shuttle** lives in Cornwall. Her most recent publication is *Will You Walk a Little Faster?* (Bloodaxe, 2017) • **Katharine Towers** has published two poetry collections with Picador; *The Remedies* was shortlisted for the 2016 T.S. Eliot Prize • **Jack Underwood**'s debut collection *Happiness* (Faber & Faber, 2015) won the Somerset Maugham Award • **Vishvantara** lives in a Buddhist residential community in London, and works as a piano teacher • **Mark Waldron**'s most recent collection is *Meanwhile, Trees* (Bloodaxe, 2016). In 2014 he was selected as a Next Generation Poet by the Poetry Book Society.

Permissions: 'The Word That Is a Prayer' by Ellery Akers © Ellery Akers, from *The Place That Inhabits Us* (Sixteen Rivers Press, 2010). Reproduced by permission of the publishers. 'Reporting Back to Queen Isabella' by Lorna Goodison © Lorna Goodison, from *Collected Poems* (Carcanet, 2017). Reproduced by permission of the publishers.